COLLABORATION
IN **LEARNING**

COLLABORATION IN LEARNING

Transcending the classroom walls

MAL LEE AND LORRAE WARD

ACER PRESS

First published 2013
by ACER Press, an imprint of
Australian Council *for* Educational Research Ltd
19 Prospect Hill Road, Camberwell
Victoria, 3124, Australia

www.acerpress.com.au
sales@acer.edu.au

Text copyright © Mal Lee and Lorrae Ward 2013
Design and typography copyright © ACER Press 2013

This book is copyright. All rights reserved. Except under the conditions described in the *Copyright Act 1968* of Australia and subsequent amendments, and any exceptions permitted under the current statutory licence scheme administered by Copyright Agency Limited (www.copyright.com.au), no part of this publication may be reproduced, stored in a retrieval system, transmitted, broadcast or communicated in any form or by any means, optical, digital, electronic, mechanical, photocopying, recording or otherwise, without the written permission of the publisher.

Edited by Ronél Redman
Cover, text design and typesetting by ACER Project Publishing
Cover photographs by John Sloman
Printed in Australia by BPA Print Group

EPUB ISBN:	9781742861470
Kindle ISBN:	9781742861623

National Library of Australia Cataloguing-in-Publication data:

Author:	Lee, Malcolm, 1944-
Title:	Collaboration in learning: Transcending the classroom walls / Mal Lee and Lorrae Ward.
ISBN:	9781742861302 (pbk.)
Notes:	Includes bibliographical references and index.
Subjects:	Learning. Teaching.

Other Authors/Contributors: Ward, Lorrae.

Dewey Number: 370.1523

This book is printed on paper derived from well-managed forests and other controlled sources certified against Forest Stewardship Council® standards, a non-profit organisation devoted to encouraging the responsible management of the world's forests.

FOREWORD

Professor Glenn Finger
Dean (Learning and Teaching), Arts, Education and Law
Griffith University, Queensland, Australia

There is arguably no more important human endeavour than to learn. It follows logically that quality teaching makes a significant, positive impact on quality learning. While much has been written and theorised about learning and teaching, Mal Lee and Lorrae Ward, the authors of *Collaboration in learning: Transcending the classroom walls*, place this book within the context of our more highly sophisticated digital, networked world.

Throughout history, individuals, communities and nations have increasingly recognised the importance of selecting, transmitting, testing, constructing and creating new knowledge and new ways of knowing. Reflecting upon the most significant historical developments, humans have always invented new technologies in response to human needs or wants. There have also been the reciprocal influences of those new technologies that have shaped our ways of knowing, thinking and learning.

Once considered new and revolutionary, we have explored and capitalised upon technologies such as the printing press, radio and television by making them integral to learning and teaching. In recent times, the technology innovation cycle has shortened—and it will continue to shorten. The big trends are evident through ubiquitous connectedness, convergence, information abundance, access taking priority over ownership of content and consumerisation. To illustrate, while it took television almost 13 years to reach 50 million consumers, the iPad—after being launched in early 2010—sold more than 60 million in only two years. There are now approximately 650 000 apps in the Apple App Store, with more than 780 new apps submitted daily and more than 15 billion apps downloaded. This is indicative of the big trends impacting upon young people and how they access, manipulate, synthesise and analyse information, communicate and interact.

These important trends and influences require an educational response.

Mal Lee and Lorrae Ward have identified and understand those big trends and the opportunities and challenges they provide for all involved in learning. In this book they situate their thinking, conceptualisations and guidance within this exciting context. Specifically, they challenge current educational leaders, systems, teachers, parents and caregivers and their communities to move to the next phase of learning beyond the more traditional classrooms walls. Each chapter makes an enlightening contribution to raising our thinking about what is possible. The authors do this in an accessible style, deliberately drawing upon their own practical experiences, insights and reflections. The presentation of case studies assists teachers, in particular, to obtain ideas from the pathfinders. In this way, the authors aim for teachers globally to 'recognise the shift occurring and seek to shape it to the best advantage' (p. 4).

Recurring themes emerge throughout the book and the authors' thinking has been informed by three key influences:

- Capitalising upon a home–school nexus to bridge the divide between the communities and their schools
- The way in which schooling is evolving as learning becomes increasingly digital and networked
- Making explicit the understandings of the resources available in the homes of young people and their communities, beyond the traditional classroom walls.

As the title reflects, collaborative learning is central to the book. In the influential work, *Collaboration: How leaders avoid the traps, build common ground, and reap big results* (2009), Morten Hansen refers to 'disciplined collaboration' as the important 'leadership practice of properly assessing when to collaborate (and when not to) and instilling in people both the willingness and the ability to collaborate when required' (p. 15). Interestingly, Hansen highlights four barriers: the 'not-invented-here' barrier (we don't reach out to others); the 'hoarding' barrier (we keep things to ourselves); the 'search' barrier (we can't find what we need anywhere); and the 'transfer' barrier (we only work with people we know well). In response, Hansen suggests that there are three levers to overcome these barriers that highlight collaboration, namely the 'Unification lever' to get everyone aiming at a lofty goal; the 'T-shape lever' to work within and across units simultaneously; and the 'Networks lever' to get people to use their personal networks. The authors provide guidance that aligns with Hansen's thinking. They outline the importance of vision, projects, programs, outputs, outcomes and the benefits. Key questions are asked in relation to these and proposals are suggested in this book. Collectively, these provide powerful ideas for all educators of young people, within and beyond the school.

This book prompts educators to consider where they want their school to be and why. In response, its guidance is to embrace collaborative teaching and learning so that the school is accessible and relevant to a wide audience through being networked. Lee and Ward argue appropriately that this vision will result in benefits through improvements in learning outputs and outcomes. By outlining the evolution of paper-based to digital schools, through to early networking and to becoming a networked school, this simple yet powerful conceptualisation provides the reader with the way forward.

To conclude, this book underlines my belief that there is nothing more important than learning and teaching. Given its recurring emphasis on the new and emerging digital networked technologies available to enhance and transform learning and teaching, it also reflects my belief that there has never been a better time to teach. By engaging with this book, I am confident that the reader will understand that networked technologies accompanied by collaboration enable opportunities to design quality, effective learning and teaching environments.

While we can, and should, always reflect and build upon our knowledge of what has worked before, there are some exciting uncharted journeys to be navigated as we progress in the twenty-first century. Through highlighting collaborative learning and teaching in this networked world, this book can assist all educators of young people—at home, within the community and at school—in charting the course to the future of learning.

Professor Glenn Finger is recognised at the institutional, state, national and international levels for improving learning and teaching through the use of new and emerging information and communication technologies. He draws upon his considerable experience as a teacher, school leader, academic and researcher to inform further research, policy and practice.

CONTENTS

Foreword	v
Figures and tables	xiii
Acknowledgements	xiv

1 Collaboration in learning: the beginnings of an idea — 1

Collaboration beyond the school	2
The great divide: communities and their schools	4
The evolution of schooling	5
The stages of evolution	7
Resources beyond the school gates	9
Collaborative teaching	10
The first steps	12
Conclusion	13

2 Discovering collaboration: the search for examples — 15

Our approach	16
The case study schools	16
The evolutionary journey of the case study schools	19
Conclusion	20

3 Learning from the pathfinders — 21

The building blocks	21
Learning from the case study experiences	25
Conclusion	30

CONTENTS

4 The many faces of collaboration — 32

Using the resources beyond the school gates — 33
Using the community as a teaching space — 35
Authentic and inquiry-based learning experiences — 35
Providing authentic audiences — 36
Collaboration across the professional school-based teaching community — 37
Collaborating with other professionals — 37
Collaboration with other schools and students — 39
Collaboration with the families — 39
Conclusion — 41

5 Collaborative teaching: a vision for the future — 43

A definition of collaborative teaching — 44
The potential teachers in a child's life — 46
Collaborative teaching explained — 47
Schooling in a collaborative world — 48
The importance of the digital in realising the vision — 49
The role of government and its authorities — 50
Conclusion — 50

6 The evidence for collaboration — 52

Parents as teachers — 53
Grandparents as teachers — 56
Students as their own teachers — 57
The benefits of collaboration — 59
Student attainment and home–school collaboration — 59
Bring your own technology (BYOT) — 61
The potential for personalised learning — 61
Bridging the divide — 62
Streamlining and improving teaching — 63
Conclusion — 65

7 Getting ready for collaboration · · · · · 66
How ready are schools? · · · · · 67
The importance of the digital · · · · · 68
Normalising the digital in the school · · · · · 70
Equitable access · · · · · 72
The readiness of the professional educators · · · · · 73
The readiness of the other teachers to collaborate · · · · · 75
Conclusion · · · · · 78

8 Putting collaboration into practice · · · · · 79
The strategy · · · · · 80
Making collaboration a reality · · · · · 82
Conclusion · · · · · 91

9 An ever-evolving development · · · · · 92
But at the beginning · · · · · 93
Educational focus · · · · · 93
Networked mindset · · · · · 94
Dismantling the school walls · · · · · 95
Empowering all your teachers · · · · · 95
The lead role of professional teachers · · · · · 96
The impact of normalised support and training · · · · · 97
Rising expectations · · · · · 97
Time to reflect · · · · · 98
Refining the teaching · · · · · 98
Riding the megatrends · · · · · 99
The pragmatics of collaboration · · · · · 100
Conclusion · · · · · 101

10 Realising the benefits of collaboration — 102

- Schools as complex organisations — 102
- Why 'benefits realisation'? — 104
- Realising benefits through the integration of multiple projects — 106
- Reflecting on your vision — 108
- What will happen when we implement the vision? — 108
- Measuring the benefits — 110
- Monitor, review, evaluate and reflect — 111
- Conclusion — 112

11 Collaboration in learning: bringing it all together — 113

- A vision for collaboration — 113
- Normalising the digital — 114
- A visionary leader is vital — 115
- The importance of supporting the professional teachers — 115
- Support of and for the other teachers — 116
- Putting the benefits at the centre — 117
- It won't be easy and it will take time — 118
- Conclusion — 118

Bibliography — 120
Index — 124

FIGURES AND TABLES

Figure 1.1	Stages in the evolutionary journey towards collaborative teaching	9
Figure 2.1	Diverting from the main route: possible side journeys	20
Figure 5.1	The *Collaboration in Learning* wheel	46
Figure 10.1	From outputs to benefits	106
Figure 10.2	Making the connections between projects	107
Table 2.1	The case study schools	17

ACKNOWLEDGEMENTS

The authors would like to thank Professor Glenn Finger of Griffith University in Queensland, Australia for the writing of the Foreword and for the wonderful support he has provided both of us over many years in researching the evolution of schooling, the impact of digital technology on that development and the effect the normalised use of the digital has had upon the teaching of young people.

When venturing into uncharted territory, it takes a particular type of leader who is prepared to overcome the inevitable travails of the unknown. That leadership was evident in all the case study schools, both in the principals and in the key senior staff. It is, however, important to make particular mention of the following people, all of whom helped to provide an insight into the workings of the case study schools: Simon Clark, Tim Clark, Mary Cuming, Tim Ennion, Adrian Francis, Trevor Galbraith, Duncan Gillespie, Michael Graffin, Jess Hall, Kim Head, Jill Hobson, David Hounsell, Suzanne Korngold, Sue Lowe, Bailey Mitchell, Alwyn Poole, Ken Pullar, Rachel Roberts, Debbie Smith, Don Stevens, Marama Stewart, Bradley Tyrell and Caitlin Ward.

As always, thanks to the wonderful editorial team at ACER Press who were once again a pleasure to work with.

Mal Lee and Lorrae Ward

CHAPTER 1

COLLABORATION IN LEARNING: THE BEGINNINGS OF AN IDEA

This book emerged out of the authors' search for schools operating in the networked mode (Lee & Ward, 2012a). Through our exploratory conversations with school leaders we began to formulate an idea of collaboration, whereby all teachers work together to promote and harness the learning that is occurring not only at school, but also beyond the school gates. This notion was one of collaborative teaching, of many teachers working together with the goal of extending and enhancing the learning of young people.

We have called this book *Collaboration in learning: Transcending the classroom walls* to reflect our growing conviction that through collaboration, within and beyond schools, student learning can be enriched and extended in ways not possible within a silo-like, traditional, paper-based education model. We want to emphasise that this collaboration is about and for learning; it is focused on achieving the best possible outcomes for individual students through the purposive utilisation of all the resources available to a school and its community.

Throughout this book you will find references to normalising the digital and the networked age. While we readily acknowledge that collaboration can occur without digital tools, the power of the digital to extend communities beyond geographical and time limitations cannot be denied. It seems to us that the normalised use of the digital is an indicator of the willingness of schools to implement a model of teaching and learning that transcends the classroom walls.

COLLABORATION BEYOND THE SCHOOL

Until recently, schools across the developed world have collaborated little with their students' homes in the actual teaching of the young (Estyn, 2009; Mackenzie, 2010). They have done so even less with the wider school community or with the young people themselves. Productive partnerships between the community and schools have been rare despite the literature supporting these (OECD, 1997; de Carvalho, 2001; Gonzalez-deHass & Willems, 2003; Cowan, Swearer Napolitano & Sheriden, 2004).

However, seemingly overnight we encountered schools across the developed world beginning to dismantle the old school walls—or at least making them more permeable. They were working with other professionals outside their schools, linking their students with external experts and/or working with their students' homes and wider communities to enrich their learning experiences. Many were taking advantage of the normalised use of the digital throughout the school's community to reach beyond their classroom walls and school gates and utilise the resources available there.

In examining the stories of these pathfinder schools, we were struck by the naturalness of their efforts, the common sense being shown and the resonance between their work and a very sizeable body of educational research around educational partnerships. We were also struck by the extent to which these schools were working 'under the radar' of the wider educational discourse. We recognised that we had been provided with an insight into the probable teaching mode of the networked world. However, when we subsequently turned to the educational literature, we found no reference to the kind of collaboration for learning that these schools were displaying as they increasingly engaged with their communities.

When the literature talks of collaboration, it has to do with collaboration among professional teachers (and occasionally, students) still within the paradigm of the 'school' as we have known it to be for a very long time. It most assuredly does not entail professional teachers collaborating with their students' other teachers—their parents, grandparents, community members and the young people themselves. Nor does it appear to recognise the power of digital technologies in a networked world to alter our notions of teaching and learning, of schooling, through the development of productive partnerships with these other teachers. What we realised is that while insular, 'stand-alone' teaching has characterised the teaching of a paper-based world, collaborative teaching could well characterise that of an increasingly digital and networked world; a world where collaboration and integration are the norm; one where the old divisions and walls of the past disappear; where there is far more integration of effort and resources across the community to support student learning.

We have tried with this book to build on the insight provided, to more fully explore the nature of the teaching occurring within those pathfinding schools working within the networked mode. We wanted to understand what had readied these schools to adopt a more collaborative approach when the vast majority have not, to flesh out the benefits of the approach and to provide a possible vision for collaborative teaching in a networked schooling environment. Through re-examining the selected case studies, we feel confident enough in our thinking to suggest how you might move your school towards a more collaborative model, thereby enjoying the kind of enhanced, holistic learning we believe is possible through collaborative teaching.

We appreciate that this more collaborative approach is in its early stage. However, in a world where the nature of schooling is evolving so rapidly, where there are no guides to show the way and where there is scant opportunity for schools across the developed world to appreciate the remarkable commonality of their experiences, we believe it is important to provide everyone who has an interest in teaching young people with an understanding of what is achievable in every school.

In today's hectic world, sadly those with a vested interest in teaching become (often unwittingly) so preoccupied in everyday, 'normal' schooling that they don't get the chance to get a helicopter-view and examine the changing scene and to appreciate how schools can better, and differently, meet the needs of their students. Rather, they continue doing what they know, relying on outdated literature, unintentionally providing an increasingly dated and irrelevant mode of teaching and learning. Any new idea, tool or model is viewed through the paradigm of teaching that already exists in their school. The question too often asked is 'How does this fit with what we are doing?', rather than 'Does this mean we should do things differently? Does this mean what we are doing is no longer as relevant as it was?'

Such is the pace of change that works written five years ago on teaching are now outdated. There is a need to continuously question, to reflect and to develop a paradigm of schooling where flexibility, interaction and collaboration are business as usual.

Collaboration in learning is designed to provide an insight into what is possible, to showcase the potential benefits and to suggest how a school and its community might make the described shift. We have deliberately written the book to be read by all of those interested in teaching across the developed world, but in particular for classroom teachers. While trying, wherever possible, to base the observations on our case study work, we have no desire to make this an academic treatise; we'll leave that to others further along the evolutionary road. Our desire is to share our insight and reflection and to hope it helps to evolve a mode of teaching apposite for the networked world. Our hope is that teachers globally will recognise the shift that is occurring and seek to shape it to the best advantage.

In the following sections of this chapter we focus briefly on the three key influences on our thinking: the divide between the community and its schools, the evolution of schooling as it becomes increasing digital and the resources that can be found in the homes and communities of our young people. Finally, we describe our vision for collaborative teaching as we construe it, not as it is currently described in the wider literature.

THE GREAT DIVIDE: COMMUNITIES AND THEIR SCHOOLS

Today's young people are teaching themselves and learning every day, all year round. The learning might not always be ideal, but it is occurring.

Schooling occupies less than 20 per cent of that time, yet holds an inordinately powerful and singular position in the teaching and learning of young people. The other 80 per cent of the time, young people, their parents and the wider community are left to their own devices, with schools seemingly neither supporting nor utilising nor even recognising what is occurring in that time. If better use were made of even part of this teaching and learning, schools should be able to markedly enhance student attainment at no extra cost.

Despite decades of public policy urging greater home–school collaboration and concerted efforts to generate a closer working relationship, schools have generally remained highly insular organisations, operating behind their walls, often with closed classroom doors, controlling all facets of formal teaching. The collaboration between the homes and the schools across the developed world remains minimal, often non-existent. In many situations the divide might even be growing. Most home–school collaboration remains tokenistic and one-way, with the parents' contribution restricted to clerical assistance, occasional book reading or unpaid taxi driving (Estyn, 2009; Mackenzie, 2010). Homework activities are the closest many parents get to their children's formal education. Schools rarely appear to acknowledge or support what students are achieving outside the school gates.

Schools have not often recognised the vital contribution that students' other teachers—their parents, grandparents and increasingly the young people themselves—have made to their education since birth, or realised the potential of that 'other' teaching and learning to both complement and support what they are doing at school. Nor have schools readily acknowledged the role of the students in their own learning and that of their peers; they have largely dismissed the 24/7/365 teaching and learning that students are undertaking outside the school walls, often with the aid of their digital technology. As a result, schools risk becoming ever-more sidelined and irrelevant to the large percentage of a student's life that occurs when they are not at school. As a student interviewed by Green and Hannon noted: 'Well, I don't let school interfere with my education if that's what you mean.' (Green & Hannon, 2007, p. 45)

In essence, most developed societies have two separate, unconnected modes of learning: the formal mode controlled by the professionals, and the informal mode provided by the parents, the young people and the community.

THE EVOLUTION OF SCHOOLING

Many years after most industries and organisations have gone digital (Thorp, 1998), schooling globally is finally in the process of following the trend, with an increasing number of schools in turn moving to the networked mode (Lee & Finger, 2010). Increasingly, schools are utilising digital tools in their administrative, management and professional tasks. However, even today, the reality is that a number of teachers are still struggling to normalise the digital in their classroom teaching, let alone adopt a mode of teaching appropriate for the networked world.

Most schools across the developed world continue to operate behind their walls as insular, 'stand-alone' organisations, having little to do with the wider community in everyday teaching and apparently unconcerned about what students are learning beyond the school gates. There appears to be no appreciation that outside their gates the networked and global world impacts upon every facet of our lives—and that it should be allowed to do so within those gates.

In further defining this inward-facing environment, teachers generally work alone in their classroom, often behind a closed door. They are gatekeepers controlling what happens in their classroom, out of reach of even the more astute principals—a position of some power. Significantly, even collaborative teaching with colleagues is still on a relatively small scale, with most teachers opting to work alone or, at best, to share resources. Interestingly, even where efforts to deprivatise practice occur through the development of modern learning environments—such as shared learning spaces or glass walls opening the classroom to view— teachers often work to reclaim these spaces.

This focus on the classroom as a single, complete environment is true at all levels of education. Most governments have concentrated their efforts to improve schooling on the work of the teacher within the classroom. In reality, the traditional mode of teaching, with its strong focus on that relatively small portion of the students' teaching and learning time spent in the formal classroom, has all but maximised its potential. There is little room for improvement in the current insular model.

The evolution to a more networked and collaborative model (described here and in our other work [Lee & Ward, 2012a]) is relatively recent, only occurring in the pathfinding schools since the early 2000s. However, if you look at the schools nearby, you will soon see the very considerable difference in operations and outlook between those schools where all teachers in the school have normalised the use of the digital in their everyday teaching and administration and those where the teaching still relies on paper, the pen and the old teaching board and only a few teachers making concerted use of the digital.

While staff working every day with the digital can, as a group, see the educational value in using the digital to collaborate more closely with their communities, the research (Lee & Finger, 2010) indicates that those still basing their teaching around the use of paper can see no reason to change their ways. They have still to recognise the opportunities opened in the networked world. In brief, they are not ready for authentic collaboration with their homes to enhance learning. For this reason we believe the use of the digital is an indicator of the extent to which a school is willing and able to look beyond its gates.

Interestingly, the transformation in thinking that occurs when the majority of teachers normalise the use of the digital in their teaching and are fortunate enough to have a principal who is prepared to lead can be rapid and dramatic. Schools can do an about-face in their thinking within a year (Lee & Finger, 2010). Why that should be so has yet to be researched, but it is evidenced in all the case studies. What we do know is that when organisations go digital and networked, whether they are banks, travel agents, post offices or schools, they move from a world of relative constancy and continuity to one of ongoing evolution and often rapid change, strongly impacted by the ever-developing technology. Most importantly, they move out of their insular, walled operations and become part of a world where collaboration and networking become the norm and the physical place ceases to be all-important.

What is remarkable today, even with schools within the one education authority, is the magnitude of the difference between those still operating in the traditional paper-based mode and those, like the case study schools, beginning to operate within a networked paradigm. When the heads of the latter schools talk to those working in the traditional mode about the educational opportunities they are pursuing in the networked paradigm, they might as well be speaking a different language, such is the difference in outlook.

It is this outlook that we believe drives them towards a collaborative model of teaching and learning. As they look ever outward, they begin to realise the potential for enriching the learning of their students; they come to recognise and appreciate the educative capacity that is outside their school gates.

THE STAGES OF EVOLUTION

Evidence from earlier work such as Lee and Finger (2010) and the literature strongly suggests there are some checkpoints along the way that will highlight how far a school is on their evolutionary journey from a paper-based model. We suggest that these checkpoints also indicate how willing and ready a school is to adopt a collaborative approach to the facilitation of learning.

One could, quite rightly, argue that it is possible to network without digital technologies; that face-face collaboration is powerful. However, the school leaders we have spoken to are clear that those teachers who are willing to operate in a networked world are also those who are willing to use digital technologies in the classroom. They are looking beyond the traditional paradigm of teacher, 'blackboard', desks and chairs within four walls. They know more is needed and that digital technologies open up a much wider environment for teaching and learning.

In an earlier study (Ward, Robinson & Parr, 2005), Lorrae found that secondary school teachers who were willing to utilise digital technologies in transformational ways were those who had broad constructions of their role in educating students. These teachers looked beyond the norm, for solutions to the problems of teaching and learning that they were facing. Digital technologies were part of their solution. Similarly, our case study schools are looking beyond the traditional model of schooling and finding solutions in not only digital technologies but also the community outside their school gates. The use of the digital is the first manifestation of their desire to solve problems of practice with innovative solutions.

We used the checkpoints below in our interviews, asking each of the school leaders to place themselves on a continuum, from paper-based to fully networked. We believe these checkpoints have value for all schools wanting to judge where they are at on an evolutionary journey from a paper-based to a networked mode.

- **Paper-based**: The majority of teachers in a school are mainly using paper, pens and the teaching board (be it black, green or white) in their everyday teaching. This was still the norm in the vast majority of the classrooms of the OECD in 2009 (Lee & Winzenried, 2009).
- **Early digital**: Around 60–70 per cent of teachers are using the digital in their everyday teaching and, as such, are nearing the critical mass stage and 'digital take-off' (Lee & Gaffney, 2008).
- **Digital**: All the teaching staff have normalised the use of the digital in their everyday teaching, but the school is still operating as a discrete, 'stand-alone' entity primarily within the traditional school walls.
- **Early networked**: The staff have normalised the use of the digital in their everyday teaching and are beginning to use the networks to operate outside the school walls and the normal school hours, and starting to 'teach' more collaboratively with the students and their homes—educationally and/or administratively—and the wider networked community (Lee & Finger, 2010).

- **Networked**: The staff have normalised the use of the digital in their everyday teaching and are collaborating authentically with all the parties inside and outside the school walls—professionally and non-professionally—in the 24/7/365 teaching of young people.

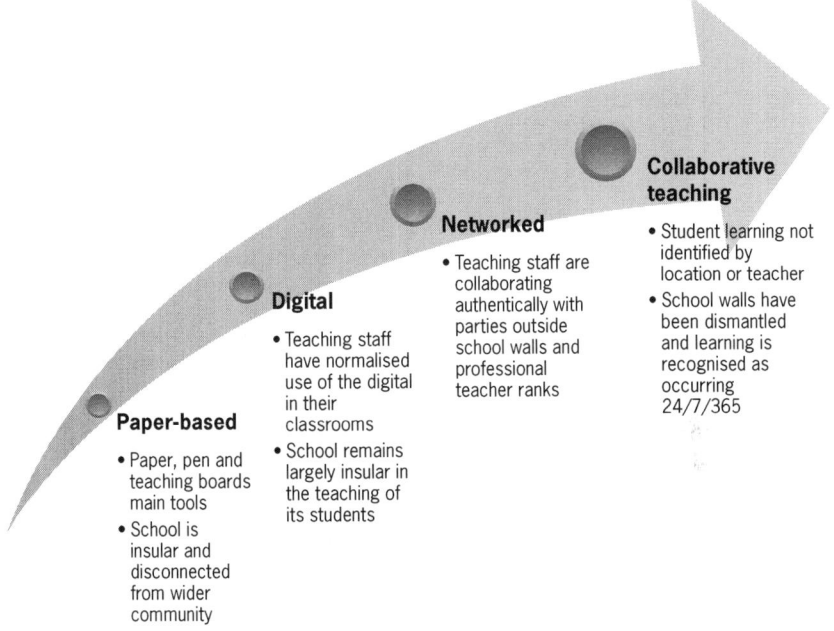

Figure 1.1 *Stages in the evolutionary journey towards collaborative teaching*

RESOURCES BEYOND THE SCHOOL GATES

While most classrooms continue to operate in a paper-based, insular paradigm, the educative capacity of students and their homes is burgeoning in the networked world outside the school. Historically, developed societies have never had such an educated group of parents and, vitally, grandparents. Significantly, particularly with the increasing number of Net Generation parents, nations have never had so many parents using the digital in every part of their lives and work, increasingly aware of its potential and being able to assist in its astute use in the teaching of young people (Lee & Finger, 2010).

Moreover, we all know the kind of digital technology available in virtually every student's home and increasingly in our and our children's hands, and the educative power of that technology (Lee & Finger, 2010). Both the parents and the students are now digitally empowered and, as the 2010 Project Tomorrow survey revealed (Project Tomorrow, 2011; 2012), many want to collaborate with their schools and would like to see their children using their own technology in the classroom teaching.

Every parent with a young child understands the importance of the digital in their lives, the way most have normalised its use 24/7/365 and the extent to which they use that technology, often in conjunction with their peers (Green & Hannon, 2007; Tapscott, 2009) to teach themselves and to shape their development. We also know how the digital technology has flattened the world (Friedman, 2006), dismantled so many of the old strict divisions of responsibility and silo-like operations and provided us with the facility to communicate instantly and inexpensively. And yet, despite all this understanding and appreciation of the potential of the digital world, there remains strong support across all levels of the education sector for a model of teaching still strongly insular and limited in time and place. The reality is that in its present form this model has little facility for significant improvement.

Let us be clear: we believe that schools and teachers are fundamental to enhancing the quality and effectiveness of the nation's education system. We are not suggesting that schools are redundant per se. The concern is that schools are using a model of teaching designed for the Industrial Age and not a networked world and, as such, the potential contribution of all teachers is being limited. We are suggesting that if schools adopt a more collaborative approach, where the professional teacher's expertise could be used to complement and support the teaching of the others educating our young people, one could improve student attainment both in and outside the classroom. If we extend the contribution of even a portion of the underdeveloped and underused 80 per cent, the improvement in student attainment could be marked. But for that to happen, the schools need to genuinely collaborate with their communities and recognise that learning occurs that is outside their control.

COLLABORATIVE TEACHING

It is too early to present a definitive definition of collaborative teaching—and indeed it may be that one can never be formed. To do so risks limiting its potential—there are many possible forms of collaborative teaching, many ways in which it can be implemented and many possible combinations of teachers. However, at its simplest, collaborative teaching is any type of teaching that involves a teacher working with other teachers, professionally or non-professionally, in the conscious teaching of young people. This conscious teaching does not need to be synchronous, nor does it need to be in a bounded context. The power of collaborative teaching lies in its holistic approach, its recognition that teaching and learning has always occurred 24/7/365 in the lives of our young people.

In the digital and networked age our capacity to harness that teaching and learning, to integrate it across time and space, has never been greater. Where once it was difficult to bridge the different contexts in which our young people learn, it is now surprisingly simple—and becoming increasingly so. It is this potential to collaborate and interact with the world outside the classroom that the pathfinding schools are increasingly realising as they develop and grow their own networks.

Collaborative teaching recognises that different teachers should have prime responsibility for teaching the various educational building blocks at different stages of young people's development. While it sounds trite, it also recognises that the sum of that teaching, in terms of the learning that is possible, is greater than any one part can achieve alone. Focusing only on what students can learn at school will not achieve the outcomes desired in the twenty-first century and needed for success in an increasingly global, competitive and demanding world. Focusing instead on ensuring a complementary, supportive and collaborative teaching paradigm has far greater potential for success.

Collaborative teaching does not differentiate between formal teachers, parents, students and their peers and those in the community who work with our young people. All have a role to play in their development, in ensuring they are able to succeed to their potential. For example, while the family is primarily responsible for the first couple of years of the child's life and for the teaching of certain social skills, a professional maths teacher ought to handle the teaching of calculus.

The approach recognises that in many (if not most) areas of learning, young people will best be taught when all the teachers work together and complement and support each other in developing a skill. Reading is an obvious example. The responsible caregivers must play a lead role in the early years, and from very early on the extended family, siblings and friends fulfil a supporting role. As the child goes to school, the professional teacher must play a significant role, in addition to the roles fulfilled by the child's other teachers. Similarly, the development of a key twenty-first century skill like collaboration can profitably be taught by all those teachers, plus those managing the 'teams' or groups the child is in and, in time the employer for whom the young person will be doing work experience.

As will become apparent as you read this book, the case studies provide an important insight into the seemingly natural inclination occurring in those schools working in the networked mode to bridge the current home–school divide and to adopt a far more collaborative approach. While there are some very exciting and important initiatives underway, we believe the case studies are only the beginning of a significant development in the history of school teaching. They provide a glimpse of the potential and highlight the diversity of possible approaches. They also exemplify why providing one vision, or definition, of collaborative teaching is problematic.

As our appreciation of collaborative teaching grows, as schools' expectations and those of their communities rise, as the technology becomes ever-more sophisticated, and as the schools bond more closely with their communities, so too will the nature of collaborative teaching and the potential learning outcomes evolve and transform. The pathfinders described here provide a guide and a glimpse of a possible future, not an endpoint. In a sense, even the pathfinders are only at first base.

In this book our primary focus is on collaboration between the school and its immediate community; on ways in which working with the community can enrich what a school offers its students. The school, and what occurs within its context, is our prime concern. This is the stage our pathfinders are at. However, in Chapter 5 we briefly step outside this frame and look forward to a time when schools are no longer the central point of learning; to a time when the child is the central point and the world around that child is aligned in ways that maximise the child's potential. Then, and only then, will we achieve personalised learning—and personalised learning environments.

THE FIRST STEPS

One has to question from the outset the vision one has for collaboration and, importantly, continue asking that question as one becomes more proficient in its use. In envisioning any future form of collaboration, it is vital that you approach the challenge working in a networked mindset and not in the mindset of the traditional, insular, paper-based paradigm. In the traditional mindset, teachers automatically ask 'What resources have we been provided to do the job?' In the networked mindset, they ask 'What resources are there in our community and the world beyond that we can bring into play? What do we want to do, rather than what can we do with what we have?' Their immediate surroundings and resources don't constrain either the teaching that occurs or the learning that is possible.

It is a challenging change in thinking. The natural inclination in a busy world is to default to the old ways. You are, for example, going to have to constantly ask 'Why are we teaching it this way?' The old way might end up being best, but you are going to have to question the teaching of all attributes like never before. In a networked world where attendance at a physical place is no longer essential to teaching and learning, you will need to ask such seemingly outlandish questions as 'Who is best placed to teach that particular attribute, and where?', recognising that it might not be the professional teacher working in a classroom.

What needs to be understood from the outset is that the traditional home–school divide and excluding parents and students from being part of the game for many generations are going to take time and deed to remedy. There will be many parents whose experiences with schools will make them very reluctant to collaborate with any school. Your communities will need to come to see the school as a focal point, as a place owned and supported by all. Your school will need to demonstrate over time that it is genuine in its desire to collaborate.

As you reflect more fully on the possible forms of collaboration described in Chapter 5, and as you note the work of the pathfinders and better understand the supporting research and the potential benefits of shifting to a more collaborative style of teaching, it is hoped that you will secure a clearer understanding of the ideal and that collaboration can enhance the learning of all young people in the networked world.

CONCLUSION

We must reiterate that these are early days. This book is the first examination of a mode of teaching and learning most in the world have not yet known, one that has the potential to be the way of the networked world. However, as you work your way through the chapters, you will appreciate that an immense amount of thinking, practical application and research will be needed before collaborative teaching begins to release its immense potential.

CHAPTER 2

DISCOVERING COLLABORATION: THE SEARCH FOR EXAMPLES

In writing this book, we have drawn on three sources of inspiration: our own vision for schooling and teaching in the networked age, the relevant literature and the exciting journeys being undertaken by the case study schools. The latter give us hope for a future where learning is no longer defined solely as that which happens in school and where it is the preserve of the professionals. In this future, both learning and the learning environment are personalised and there is a holistic approach to the development of our young people. We readily acknowledge the 'nirvana-like' qualities of our vision in Chapter 5. However, we believe the case study schools show that it can be a reality.

In the following chapters, we describe what we learned from the case study schools. In some instances we supplement our case study evidence with that from the literature. Constraints of time and space made it difficult to talk to as many schools as we would have liked. Further, as evidenced in the case studies, even these pathfinders are in the early stages of being networked; there is still much they need to learn and achieve. The literature is another guide to the way forward.

In this chapter, we describe our approach to collecting examples of collaboration to share. We also describe the case study schools in general demographic terms in order to provide a context for the rest of the book.

OUR APPROACH

We wanted examples of schools that were moving towards a more collaborative model of teaching and learning. We wanted schools that were in the process of opening their doors and increasingly working with the wider community to enrich the learning of their students. We wanted to better understand what drives these pathfinders, these explorers, to move away from the 'safe', well-known and mapped traditional world. We also wanted to better understand their journeys so that others could follow more readily.

We used a semi-structured interview format, ensuring that we asked each school the same questions, including where they thought their school sat on the evolutionary continuum described in the first chapter. The interviews were undertaken by Skype and in most instances recorded. Findings from these interviews have been collated under thematic areas of interest in the relevant chapters of this book and provide the models of practice in Chapter 4.

In our search for case studies we 'travelled' to the United Kingdom, the United States, Australia and New Zealand. The school leaders we talked to all shared a common desire to share their story and to reflect on their journey. All were open about the challenges they face and about the hard work of being a pathfinder. And they were all equally optimistic and excited about what was being achieved and where their journey was taking them.

THE CASE STUDY SCHOOLS

In total, we spoke to school leaders at 16 schools. Their stories are told throughout this book, providing insights into their journeys and highlighting the individual natures, the importance of school leadership and the necessity of the digital. All are at different stages of their journey; some have different endpoints in sight. We hope you will be able to take something from each and map your own journey forward.

Table 2.1 is a summary of the key demographics of the case study schools. Of concern for us is that the schools we have included are all from middle to high socioeconomic communities (SES). Beyond this concern we are satisfied that we have covered a range of school types, sizes and locations.

DISCOVERING COLLABORATION: THE SEARCH FOR EXAMPLES

Table 2.1 The case study schools

SCHOOL	COUNTRY	SES	LOCATION	TYPE	AUTHORITY	SIZE	STAGE
Apiti	NZ	High	Rural	Primary	Government	Very small: 30	Early networked
Balmacewen	NZ	High	Urban	Interm. (7, 8)	Government	Medium: 500	Digital
Broulee Public	Australia	Middle	Regional	Primary	Government	Medium: 300	Early networked
Coal Mountain Elementary	USA	High	Urban	Primary	Government	Large: 880	Early networked
Concordia	Australia	High	Urban	Secondary	Independent	Large: 800	Early digital
Corpus Christi	Australia	Middle	Urban	Secondary	Catholic	Large: 1000	Digital
Forsyth Central	USA	High	Urban	Secondary	Government	Large: 2000	Early networked
The Friends' School	Australia	High	Urban	K–12	Independent	Large: 1300	Early networked
Kimi Ora	NZ	High	Urban	Special	Government	Very small: 30	Early networked
Kolbe	Australia	Middle	Urban	Secondary	Catholic	Large: 1000	Early networked
Mt Hobson	NZ	High	Urban	Middle (7–10)	Independent	Very small: 50	Early networked
Noadswood	UK	High	Urban	Secondary	Government	Large: 1100	Early networked
Pukeokahu	NZ	High	Rural	Primary	Government	Very small: 11	Early networked
South Forsyth	USA	High	Urban	Secondary	Government	Large: 1600	Early networked

17

Two of our participants are not individual schools. Rather, they are the host school for a collaborative venture among schools utilising a virtual learning network. As such they are not included in the demographic table below.

- The Virtual Learning Network (primary) is included as a case study of the potential of the networked age to enable schools to share resources and to collaborate in the teaching of their students despite the market forces that can cause competition among schools.
- The Global Classroom Project shows what can be achieved when teachers and students are able to work across international boundaries. This is a global collaboration community that focuses on international student and teacher collaboration and cultural exchanges. It enables individual teachers to work beyond their classroom walls even if the rest of the school is not ready to make the shift.

The majority of the schools are from major urban cities within their respective countries, one is from a regional city (minor urban) and two others are from small, isolated rural communities. Within the two communities described above there is a wide mix of schools in terms of location. There is, moreover, a mix of government, Catholic and independent schools, with varying degrees of school autonomy ranging from those from highly centralised systems through to those with considerable independence. There is also a mix of primary and secondary schools, with one school for students with such high special education needs that regular schooling is not an option.

Finally, none of the case study schools saw themselves as fully networked. Some reported as being digital, others as early networked—that is, they were moving towards a networked model and the use of the digital was common, if not ubiquitous, in their schools.

None of the variables displayed in Table 2.1 appears to define the nature of collaboration occurring. It is true that most of the schools are of high SES and in urban areas, but this should not preclude other schools from collaborating in similar ways. One could argue, as the small rural schools in New Zealand show, that there is a greater need for collaboration in smaller rural areas, and the same could be argued for lower socioeconomic school communities.

Rather, it is the similarities in vision and commitment to student learning that defines these schools. Despite differences in culture, size and community, these schools all share a commitment to their students and their communities. They are schools that are willing to take risks, to enter largely uncharted territories and, where necessary, to break with tradition. The extent to which they have done this varies, as does the current stage in their journey.

Despite their diversity, there emerged (as will become apparent in the next chapter) a very considerable commonality in the foundations of their collaboration. Indeed, in analysing those commonalities we erred on the conservative side and while there were suggestions of other similarities we held back mentioning them.

THE EVOLUTIONARY JOURNEY OF THE CASE STUDY SCHOOLS

An important message emerging from these schools is that when considering the evolution of schools, one size does not fit all. The journey described in our evolutionary stages is not predetermined, nor should it be. Importantly, all the case study schools were driven by the need to solve a problem of practice. Further, they were reflective and proactive, not accepting of the status quo; they were not waiting for someone else to solve their problems. This culture of learning, of reflection and of experimentation is driven by strong visionary leadership and by a shared desire to do better for their students.

As Chapter 4 shows, they have all gone on different journeys: some have focused on networking within the school rather than with the community or with other schools, while others have begun to work more openly with their parent community. Still others have moved to an early networked model, embracing the opportunities the wider community offers them.

When we considered their stories in more detail, it became clear that some had diverged at key stages of their journey and gone on a side road (Figure 2.1). Whether they remain there or backtrack and continue on the main highway to other checkpoints will remain to be seen. That decision will lie with their school leadership. It will, hopefully, be made based on evidence and the needs of their community.

COLLABORATION IN LEARNING

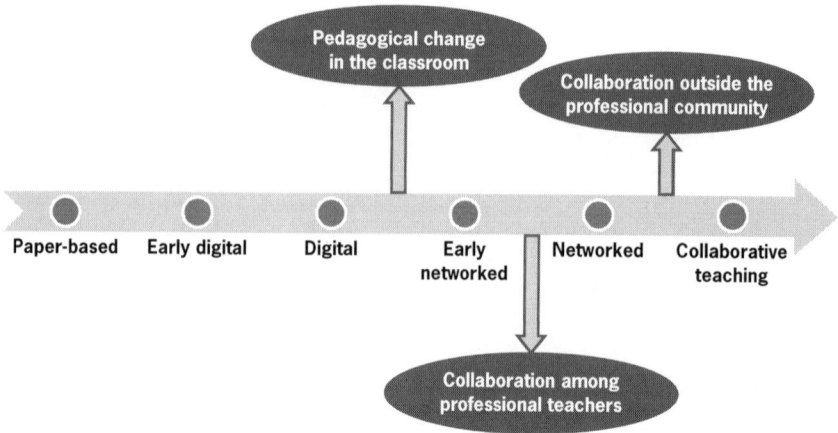

Figure 2.1 *Diverting from the main route: possible side journeys*

CONCLUSION

As a precursor to reading the rest of this book we recommend that you place your school and your staff on the aforementioned continuum, using the checkpoints we used in this study to determine where you are on the journey described by the case study experiences. Where would you sit based on the journey depicted? We also recommend that you think about the problems of practice you would like to solve and how collaboration could help solve them. Ask yourselves questions like:

- How many of your teachers are truly digital, let alone networked?
- How willing are your teachers to open the doors of their classrooms and let the outside world in?
- How open are your teachers to new ideas to solve old problems?
- To what extent do they rely on pen and paper, using digital technologies as an added extra?
- How willing is your community to work with you in the collaborative teaching of the young people?
- Do you have the necessary digital infrastructure?

These are questions you need to be asking as you consider your school's readiness, if not relevance, in the networked age. The remainder of this book will hopefully serve as a guide as you consider the future and plan your journey forward.

CHAPTER 3

LEARNING FROM THE PATHFINDERS

As we indicate in the introduction to this book, the concept of collaboration for learning, as we describe it, is still new. There are few certainties attached to it, but there is sufficient evidence to point to its growing importance and relevance as well as to what is required for its implementation. In this chapter, we briefly describe what we believe to be the building blocks for collaborative teaching before discussing a series of key themes that are particularly pertinent to the implementation of collaborative teaching—and have resonance across the case studies.

THE BUILDING BLOCKS

Each of the case study schools had the building blocks described below in place to some extent. If they were not already there, the school leadership were well aware of their necessity and working towards building the desired capacity.

A visionary leadership

The school principal is central to any shift to a more collaborative approach, not only within their own school but also to a wider uptake from the community. The key to success is an astute and visionary principal, one who is desirous of providing their students with an education for the twenty-first century, with the wherewithal to lead an increasingly complex, closely integrated and ever-evolving school (Lee & Ward, 2012b). Bluntly, without that facilitating leadership the likelihood of moving far is minimal.

In many of the case studies the development strategy articulated by senior leaders was more freewheeling and on a much larger scale than one normally hears about. These leaders were looking beyond the everyday for new opportunities to move their school forward. They were open and receptive to new ideas and to change. All understand the key learning outcome obligations the school has to meet, be it x per cent of A levels or the best possible performance on a basic skills test. All also have a more holistic 24/7/365 educational aspiration for their students—an aspiration that is firmly based in the learning needs of their students.

Willing and capable professional teachers

There is an abundance of literature regarding the necessity of professional teachers being both willing and able to change their practice for any school reform to be effective. The power of teachers as gatekeepers to their classroom is undeniable. Even the most astute principal will struggle to effect school-wide change if there is insufficient support—and understanding—among the teaching staff.

With the exception of the very small schools, all the case studies had the normal mix of teachers—a spread of early and late adopters—and several had (to use the euphemism) some 'challenging' teachers. However, there was a growing commitment among the professional staff and an increasing awareness of the importance and value of collaboration. Further, as the benefits to their school and their students became apparent, more teachers came on board. The excitement about what they were doing and their achievements to date was palpable.

The schools also had a mix of teacher digital competencies and teaching expertise. This was made even more interesting in some schools by the teachers' growing preference to use different mixes of digital tools. Not surprisingly, that difference was usually allied to their particular expertise and area of interest.

Working with the staff, supporting them and guiding them towards a more collaborative approach is an ongoing task for many of the school leaders. As new staff join the school, induction becomes critical to ensure they understand what is expected. The culture of the school and the value it places on collaboration and learning need to be regularly reinforced and celebrated. Support and recognition need to be given to the staff leading the way; support and strong guidance to those trailing behind. At Balmacewen Intermediate School there is no option but to be collaborative in their school—it is a norm of practice.

A conducive culture

It is essential that there is a *collaborative learning culture* within the school if collaborative teaching is to be implemented successfully. This is closely linked to the building block of a capable and willing teaching staff and also to that of the community beyond the school gates. Such a culture values ongoing learning, is built on trust and openness, is professional not personal and respects and values the input of all in the community.

Teachers need to be confident enough to open their practice to challenge, learn to critique others and accept criticism themselves. They also need to be reflective, consider the 'So what?' of evidence, be willing to take some risks and continuously be open to new learning. Above all, they need to be able to put aside their notions of professional autonomy and be willing to work with all the teachers of the young people. This is not as easy as it sounds.

Some of the school leaders spoken to commented on the sudden reversion under pressure to their old autocratic ways by some teachers. They also commented on changing resources, new and potentially disruptive technologies and a changing national context that could add new pressures, making collaboration more difficult. This ever-changing environment means it is essential to constantly reflect, be willing to review and revise and not let one's eyes off the ball. It also means it is essential to look after the pathfinding teachers—the risk takers.

Chapter 10 offers one model for developing such a culture.

A willing and capable community

All the case studies took time to convince their students, their homes and their community that they were genuine in their wish to collaborate. Many were also actively working to develop the capability of their community through the provision of training on digital tools and through a highly visible invitational policy that makes it clear that parents and other community members are welcome. For many schools it is about raising their profile in the community, making it clear they see the school as part of the wider community and not as a separate, walled community.

As flagged, after years of tokenistic involvement it can take time for the community to recognise that a school is (to use an Australian vernacular) 'fair dinkum' in its desire to collaborate. Even once that has occurred, the successful, sustained use of community resources takes time—and it takes the application of astute people skills by the school staff. Community elders go on holiday; families place pressures on them; sadly elders sometimes become infirm; and indeed some of the mentors, like some professional educators, can be difficult to work with. Everything won't necessarily be plain sailing and it may be necessary to provide ongoing support and professional development opportunities.

An apposite digital infrastructure

All the case study schools use an array of teaching tools—old and new—where appropriate, but they also now use many of the emerging digital resources very comfortably. Significantly, most have made or are about to make use of a 'bring your own technology' (BYOT) model.

As one would expect, all the schools have:
- teaching rooms with internet access and the requisite suite of digital technology, using either IWBs or data projectors
- all teachers with their personal mobile technology
- full network connectivity; most have wi-fi connectivity for the personal mobile technology.

Whether small or large, they also have in place a digital communications suite with which to collaborate with their community. It is a normalised part of their everyday teaching, a facility all teachers can use when appropriate. It is also suitable for their school size and needs. Interestingly, most of the schools have opted to take advantage of the cheaper options that can also be used by everyone within the homes and community.

These suites are not necessarily complex or expensive. The nature of technology today enables the acquisition of use of sophisticated technologies in ways never seen before. For example, all are built around an integrating website, but this can be no more than a wiki or a blog. Indeed, only the secondary schools appear to utilise some form of online learning platform, or what some term a VLE (virtual learning environment). The

New Zealand and Australian primary schools opted to use various mixes of the free Web 2.0 tools or the likes of Apple's wiki server. Whatever their size or nature, these suites offer the schools the facility to instantly communicate with all within the school's community—and beyond. All include some form of regular digital communication, support and advice, and all have the facility for online discussions and feedback.

While you will appreciate that the approaches taken by the schools will differ and have their own individuality, a quick look at any of the examples below will reveal much—not only about the digital communications suite the school is using, but also the nature of the collaborative teaching in place.

http://apitischoolwiki.wikispaces.com/
http://www.broulee-p.schools.nsw.edu.au/Collaborative_Schooling.html
http://www.pukeokahu.school.nz

LEARNING FROM THE CASE STUDY EXPERIENCES

In this section we discuss the key themes that came through in our discussions with the case study schools. These are experiences that were common across all the schools to some extent. They are our synthesis of the key attributes emerging from the case study experiences. We believe there are important messages within each of these for schools wishing to follow the case study schools on a collaborative teaching journey.

The normalised use of the digital

Not surprisingly, the case study schools, their homes and community have all normalised the use of the digital to some extent. As stated earlier, this seems to be not only a precursor to collaboration but also an indication of the willingness of a school to evolve, to change its teaching and learning to meet new challenges and to solve problems of practice.

The expectation of the majority of the schools is that digital tools will be used naturally in the teaching and learning occurring within and beyond the classrooms. The extent and the nature of that use are determined (as it should be) by the school's and community's vision for their young people. Interestingly, even in those schools where the digital was not immediately obvious, it soon became apparent that its use had permeated all areas of the school operations. It was just so normalised no-one bothered to mention it, and so purposive that it was only referred to in terms of the activities it was supporting.

For example, at Mt Hobson Middle School the use of the digital is understated, yet every student spends one hour a day doing independent study—at which time they have exclusive use of a networked computer, with access to the school printer and their own email account. For a recent project the students created music videos. The digital tools they used came from home, often their own smart phones. Yet this is not a BYOT school ... or is it?

Similarly, Balmacewen Intermediate would argue that the digital is not an essential part of what they do. Again, scratch beneath the surface and it is there—its use is so normalised and so purposive (rather than forced) that it is not seen as warranting a mention. It is not the focus of what they are doing; it is not the reason for the tasks being described.

Dismantling the walls

In all the schools, collaboration is (wittingly or unwittingly) dismantling the old school walls, both internal and external, and lessening the importance of the physical place in teaching and learning as the schools use a combination of the digital and face-to-face interaction in their teaching. A common feature is the currency and openness of their daily operations, whether teaching and learning or administration. Check the websites of all the case study schools and you will find they are up to date, with few of the secret passwords, cyber walls or tiredness that characterise so many other school websites. Where passwords are used, it is for the protection of the students such as attainment records or details of their special needs.

These are schools willing not only to have their daily teaching and operations openly scrutinised, but also to provide the facility for those interested to offer immediate comment and feedback via various Web 2.0 facilities and email. All are, at least in part, using open sites that provide all those interested with an insight into the school's daily activities. The contrast with the traditional approach where the school operates behind closed doors with only the occasional snapshot of the teaching, and where comment is carefully filtered before it gets outside the school gates, is pronounced. The idea of teaching being contained within the classroom walls or behind the traditional closed class door is rapidly vanishing.

Open blog use, as evidenced in the case studies, says that the leadership and the teachers are proud of their school, of the teaching that occurs there and of their students' work. It also says that the school has a principal willing to lead, it has the requisite technology, the teaching staff have largely normalised the use of the digital in their teaching, it is open to collaborating with its homes and, very importantly, it is open to immediate feedback on its work.

Compare, for example, reporting models where schools provide a list of acceptable comments for limited paper-based reports with those schools where the students' work is readily available and where their progress is recorded in an open forum. When a student writes directly onto their blog site—as occurs at Pukeokahu School—there is no hiding for the teacher concerned.

Indeed, we would argue that the open, whole-school use of class blogs is a telling indicator that the school is operating within the networked mode and is using some form of collaborative teaching. If you want to visit such a school, our recommendation is that you do your homework and look at the blog sites available for public viewing.

Multi-purpose operations

What is also interesting (and done seemingly unwittingly) is the way in which the teaching and the collaboration often serve multiple purposes, enhancing the efficiency of the teaching and containing the teachers' workload. The use of class blogs perhaps best illustrates this development. For example, the blog can simultaneously:
- work as an excellent teaching tool, stimulating a more student-centred approach where students create and post their work each day
- further collaboration with students' homes, showing what the students are working on, while at the same time flagging likely home follow-up
- promote and market the school and its work
- provide the avenue for instant home feedback and comment directly to each teacher
- aid the school's accountability to its clients and government with all being able to 'inspect' the school's operations on a daily basis.

With a little forethought and the wise use of the digital, one can use a single activity to teach multiple skills and have it serve multiple purposes.

Normalised teacher development

Not surprisingly, the case study schools generally revealed a relatively simplistic understanding of what was entailed in collaboration, and most flagged the need for concerted enhancement in the area. They were open about the fact that they were still learning, still developing and that things would continue to change. It is what one would expect when moving from a position of little or no collaboration to where it is applied every day. They were also open about the need to provide professional support and development to not only the professional teachers but also those in the wider community, particularly in the use of the digital.

Although still early days, it is interesting and refreshing to see the priority many are already attaching to the ongoing provision of support and training for all the teachers of young people—the staff, the parents, the community and the young people themselves. Significantly, all but the Forsyth County schools have taken this initiative of their own volition without any support from their education authority, government or teacher training institution.

What is noticeable is not only the quality of the early offerings, their design for their particular context, the astute use made of the various digital tools and the school's digital communications suite, but also how well others could use or amend the materials developed by the school and their particular community. All are using a mix of the online and face-to-face, and all are very aware of the magnitude of the challenge, particularly for the pathfinding schools seeking to reverse a long embedded approach of 'leave the teaching to the professionals, they know what is best'. While the challenge at the secondary level is immense, it is also considerable at the primary level. One is seeking to create a very different teaching and learning environment to that known for generations. The reality is a significant number of parents have reached the point of saying 'it is the school's job to teach, not mine', and schools appear to accept that, despite the arguments around the impact of the home environment on learning outcomes.

Consider the kind of challenge the leadership of Noadswood School has in the old, leafy streets of Portsmouth as it seeks to enhance the facility of its parents to better teach their secondary-age students the cognitive, social and emotional skills needed to succeed in their A levels. One can appreciate Dr Tim Ennion's task of convincing staff to put in the hours at the after-school small-group parent seminars. If you look at the support

Broulee Public School is providing its parents, you will get an idea of their commitment to providing this support (http://www.broulee-p.schools.nsw.edu.au/SST_Blog_Link.html).

The progress being made by these pathfinders and others is to be lauded. Their task will become that much easier when the school can demonstrate its success and other schools in the region adopt the same approach.

The unintended

Often mentioned in the interviews were the unintended outcomes that continue to flow from the adoption of a more collaborative approach, and schools suddenly being provided with extra resources from unanticipated sources, with people and organisations volunteering their support or services often out of the blue. Some of the contributions were small or were strategic alliances, but in many of the schools there have been major unintended windfalls.

Many of the leaders we spoke to were surprised how strong the perception was—even with government agencies—that schools wanted to look after themselves and did not need to collaborate beyond the school community, be it with local businesses, sporting groups, local government or grants bodies.

The role of the authorities

Significantly, but in keeping with the natural development, few of the case study schools have been prompted to make the change by their education authority or government. Rather, the impetus has come from within the school and its leadership.

Tellingly, the support of the authorities has been lacking in most jurisdictions. Their narrow focus on achievement-based standards and accountability models has probably been a deterrent for schools wishing to adopt a more collaborative and holistic model of teaching and learning. The 'grammar of bureaucracy', the long-accepted norms of reporting and accountability, can be an impediment to change. It is beyond the scope of this book to debate the merits of either model—or even whether they are mutually exclusive (which we doubt, as evidenced by the case studies). Suffice here to say that currently schools are being constrained by the need to meet paper-based demands and are becoming increasingly risk-averse.

Forsyth County in Georgia, USA is one of the exceptions and serves as an excellent example of how a knowing education authority can both promote and support a shift to a more networked and collaborative model of teaching and learning. One of the longer-term challenges (which we address briefly in this book) is how governments and authorities can work with schools to facilitate what has to be a school initiative in a way where the approach becomes the norm with all schools. Encouraging schools to work together through the facilitation of learning networks, along with minimising the demands on schools to provide long-term plans and to meet paper-based bureaucratic requirements, is a good starting point.

Two of the case study schools have commented on issues with the authorities: on tensions between their visions and the expectations of the authorities regarding paper work; and a narrower focus than the school considers ideal. It is such tensions that limit innovation in a time where innovation is needed. More of the same will not solve the problems plaguing education systems around the world.

Just as we have argued that schools need to work with their communities in making changes, they also need to work with the authorities. This may be more difficult. It requires both sides to work together, to talk and to make compromises. It requires the school to provide evidence of success and the authorities to have the capacity to understand what the school is trying to achieve. Also important is for authorities to understand the courage it takes for a school to attempt to move outside the norm. They must support them in that move, celebrate their successes and learn from their mistakes. When making judgements on a school, they need to be willing to listen, to understand what the school is trying to do and work with them to find compromises where necessary.

CONCLUSION

In identifying the aforementioned commonalities and building blocks, we were conservative in our reading of the trends. There were hints of other common developments and glimpses of where the schools would soon be travelling, but as yet the evidence was not strong enough to include in this book.

What is apparent, as mentioned, is for everyone to recognise that it is early days. An immense amount of developmental work has yet to be done, all are only beginning to think and work in the networked mode and in the coming years they will be seeking to fully realise the potential of collaboration that is focused on enhancing learning that transcends the classroom and embraces the world beyond.

CHAPTER 4

THE MANY FACES OF COLLABORATION

In Chapter 3, we used our findings from the case study research to describe the building blocks that are required for collaborative teaching, to highlight the need for a concerted effort from all in education—the authorities, the schools and the community—and to emphasise the importance of a school culture that values openness and transparency—one where not just the classroom walls but also the school walls are dismantled.

The many forms collaboration can validly take are apparent from even this relatively small sample of case studies. The limiting variable (beyond the building blocks) is the human mindset. In this chapter, we look more specifically at the different models or approaches to collaboration we found across the case study schools. In some instances, the differences in implementation are a feature of the stage they are at in their journey; in others they are a reflection of the different contexts within which they operate and the varying needs of their students.

The embryonic nature of collaborative teaching and the often isolated context within which the pathfinders are working means that each is implementing their own changes and charting their own journey towards greater collaboration in learning. The result is that, while they share a common desire to enhance the teaching and learning within their schools and to look beyond the school gate, they are all doing so differently. We trust that this rich array of collaboration will motivate other schools and teachers to think about what they, too, can achieve and that, by looking beyond their school and collaborating with others, there is something that points to the next stage in their own journey.

USING THE RESOURCES BEYOND THE SCHOOL GATES

An important outcome for schools operating in the networked mode and beginning to work more collaboratively with their homes and community is the sudden swell in teaching resources they experience. Broulee Public School, an Australian state primary school catering for a small regional beach-side community, is an excellent example of this. Socioeconomically the school is pretty much on the Australian norm. It was struggling to provide its students with the learning experiences the principal believed were essential for the twenty-first century. Reaching out to the community for support proved more valuable than was initially anticipated. The result has been an increase in specialist teachers within the school, additional equipment as the students increasingly provide their own technology and funding from a range of sources.

Virtually overnight, the school has moved its teaching and programs from being adequately to being richly resourced. The following list clearly depicts the depth of the resources gained.

- A cross-section of student mentors drawn from its parent ranks and the community elders.
- The provision of home internet access to those few students who did not have this facility and an iPad for a boy without an arm, through liaison with several community and service groups.
- Clerical support for the school's iCentre—the integration of its old separate library and ICT operations.
- Two music specialists to run a school choir with the help of the local University of the Third Age (U3A).
- A community band program, where previously there had been none, where the students provide their own instruments.
- Three community members, an educational author, a graphic artist and a parent who take responsibility for providing weekly advice articles and support to the parents, grandparents and interested community on the aforementioned building blocks.
- A parent group with whom the school is working in the collaborative

24/7/365 teaching of the identified core educational building blocks, using, in the main, the digital resources of the students' homes.
- A multifaceted, multi-way digital information and communications suite built on the technology of the homes, community and school that provides the school's community with ready, inexpensive open access to all its activities.
- A special grant to enable the school to showcase its collaborative schooling approach and use of the digital with other schools.
- A free staff team-building program offered to the school as the result of its collaboration with and support for the organisation involved.
- A graduated shift to a BYOT mobile resourcing model where the senior students use their own mobile technology in class, thus releasing the previously allocated funds for other programs.
- A closer bond with the region's main tertiary education faculty.
- Closer ties with the village sporting groups running complementary, non-competing activities.
- Support of the local U3A, the shire's senior computer users group, the dune care organisation and the shire's environmental support group.

Broulee Public School's jigsaw representation of its integration of these resources, available at http://www.broulee-p.schools.nsw.edu.au/Collaborative_Schooling.html, provides an insight into the way the school is managing its increased teaching resources.

Importantly, the new resources have served to reinforce to the staff the importance of adopting a more networked mindset and of considering at all times who and what can be added. As the teachers have come to see the benefits for their students, they have increasingly supported the principal as she implements new ideas and resources. Further, as word has spread, members of the community continue to come forward to support the school.

Similar things can be seen at other schools such as Balmacewen Intermediate where the community are used as experts to support student projects. For example, one parent provided expert guidance to students during a sustainability project. In another, a photographer was brought in to work with the students on a documentary-based project. Also in New Zealand, at Pukeokahu School, the local community, rich in artists and musicians, offers support to the school; at Mt Hobson Middle School, the principal regularly utilises guest speakers to share stories of personal experiences in order to motivate and inspire the students.

USING THE COMMUNITY AS A TEACHING SPACE

A slightly different model to bringing the experts and resources into the school can be found at Mt Hobson Middle School. This is a small independent school operating out of an old villa. The school itself has limited infrastructure and space. Rather than investing in expensive equipment, facilities and resources, the students utilise what is already available in the community.

Mt Hobson's teachers teach the academic subjects plus technology and art. For sport, drama, music, dance and other activities, the students go out to the community and access experts in the field. For example, in a recent study of the human circus, the Year 8 students spent two afternoons learning to fly on a trapeze.

While there will be a cost attached in some instances, this needs to be balanced against the ongoing costs of purchasing, maintaining and replacing equipment and facilities. Further, the students are able to access not only expert guidance from specialist tutors, but also specialised facilities. Maybe there is a dance academy or a local sports club or music school that could work with your school, allowing your school-based teachers to focus on other areas of teaching and learning—and improving the student experience.

AUTHENTIC AND INQUIRY-BASED LEARNING EXPERIENCES

One of the very early stages of collaborative teaching is the provision of authentic and inquiry-based learning experiences for students. Such learning experiences are centred on real-life situations and contexts, involving the students in solving problems of real life and encouraging them to participate fully in the world outside their school.

One example of this is the learning at Apiti School; another is at Balmacewen Intermediate. In both schools, much of the learning is experiential in nature; it is also based in real situations that the students can relate to. For example, at Apiti School, the students built bird boxes (technology) that were then put into the school grounds. The students recorded the number of birds that used the boxes and were in their grounds as a result (graphing and statistics). With the knowledge that an insect is destroying pasture in the local area, the project was seen as a way of enabling the students to support the local community by attracting birds (environmental studies). Many different forms of learning can be found in that one project. They also entered their bird boxes into the local agricultural show—an authentic audience for their work. At Balmacewen, the students also often work out in the community, solving problems drawn from real life.

At Mt Hobson, the students all undertake independent learning in the form of comprehensive projects that they complete over a five-week period. The projects are thematic and involve different core skills such as writing, research, mathematics and science. The students work on their own with the support of the teachers; the topics are diverse and interesting and they engage the students in learning that extends their understanding.

PROVIDING AUTHENTIC AUDIENCES

Closely linked to the above is the value to be found in providing your students with authentic audiences for their work. Examples of this can be found at both Pukeokahu and Apiti schools. These schools are in small rural communities where the students have limited opportunities to gain critique and feedback on their work.

Students are able to show the world what they are doing through their blogs and wikis. The Pukeokahu students write directly onto their blogs. They rarely use books—their working space is online. The principal at Pukeokahu School twitters other principals when her students have put new work up so they can tell their students to read it. The Apiti students have learning blogs with a wide range of work displayed, providing not only a record of their learning but also an online gallery for others to view.

Students at both schools also display their work in the community in a physical sense. At Apiti School, the students take every opportunity to showcase their learning, such as singing at the local hotel for the senior citizens from the community or displaying their art in a local shop. At Pukeokahu School, the students created a movie that was premiered in the movie theatre of a nearby town. They also have a public art show in the local community. Both principals spoke of the motivation through the provision of a wide audience for the students, and of the increase in the quality of the students' work and the resultant pride in what they produced and in their school.

COLLABORATION ACROSS THE PROFESSIONAL SCHOOL-BASED TEACHING COMMUNITY

While it would seem obvious for teachers to do so, given the connected and networked age we live in, genuine collaboration across the professional community is not as common as one might expect. Initiatives such as the Network Learning Communities in New Zealand (Ward & Henderson, 2011) and the Collaborative Learning Communities in Ontario (Vause & Cameron, 2012) highlight the potential of professional interaction and collaboration to support the enhancement of teaching and learning. However, for those teachers still operating in the paper-based mode the natural inclination remains to work behind closed doors, accessing the internet for resources but not openly collaborating and sharing with others. Recent research undertaken in New Zealand (Ward & Marentette, 2012) highlights how limited professional collaboration really is, both in nature and extent; student collaboration is even more limited.

As a result, schools such as Balmacewen Intermediate work hard to ensure that professional collaboration within their school is part of the school culture. It is the expectation (not an option) at Balmacewen that the staff will collaborate. It is also mandated that they become involved with the community and not just the other teaching staff; they must be willing to work with others.

The Virtual Learning Network (VLN) in New Zealand is a successful example of teachers sharing ideas and resources through social networking. The network is a meeting place for teachers from across the country with different communities, based around specific areas of interest and need. It is also a repository for resources. The VLN has no structures or boundaries and is continuously changing and growing. There are a number of different communities or groups—some are closed while others are open for all to see. Visit www.vln.school.nz to have a look.

COLLABORATING WITH OTHER PROFESSIONALS

The professional collaboration examples above relate more to general professional learning activities than focused collaboration among teachers to meet the needs of individual students. Kimi Ora School in New Zealand provides an exciting example of how Web 2.0 technologies can be used to connect all the teachers of a child in a way that is focused on meeting the young person's broad educational needs. While this is a special school for those students with high special needs, it should be seen as an example of the potential of providing evidence of learning and of sharing expertise around any individual child.

The use of student blogs, video and other media along with e-portfolios has enabled the teachers at Kimi Ora to ensure that all those involved with the young people are well informed and able to participate regularly in the development of the students' learning program. This includes family, friends, special therapists and other professionals. Given the nature of the needs of these students, many of the student blogs are password protected. Interestingly, the parents of one child asked for his blog to be open to the public so proud were they and their child of his progress and what had been achieved that they wanted all to know about it.

In addition, this school has a Facebook site where caregivers can share concern, ideas and successes, and help one another meet the needs of their young people. This community is not open to the public and only friends of the school can join, which is understandable given the nature of the needs of the students and their families, but again an excellent example of the use of social media to support learning through collaboration.

The potential of Web 2.0 technologies to support students in transition between schools is, as yet, unrealised. Sending a secondary school teacher the blog addresses of students so they could see the work that had been done could be invaluable in meeting the individual needs of students. As Kimi Ora School has shown, a wealth of information can be transmitted through video and other electronic means.

Also largely unrealised is the potential to support the learning of young people with special education needs in regular schools. The support that classroom teachers need is often not immediately available; experts are generally based in urban centres and are often stretched. When they can pay a visit to the school, it may be an unnatural, time-pressured event. Utilising video of students and digital examples of work, such as at Kimi Ora, could enable a greater level of 'just in time' support in all schools.

Linked to this idea—and of using the community as a teaching space—is the use of digital technologies to bring experts to the classroom virtually. While the Mt Hobson model provides the students with a wide range of learning experiences, this is not always possible. The VLN, Broulee Public School, Concordia College and The Friends' School also provide the schools with access to experts using video conferencing and other tools such as Adobe Connect and video streaming.

COLLABORATION WITH OTHER SCHOOLS AND STUDENTS

As well as facilitating collaboration among professional teachers as described above, the VLN also facilitates collaboration among schools. The VLN (Primary) consists of a group of primary schools that teach languages collaboratively. It is worth visiting the website to gain a sense of what is being achieved: http://www.vln.school.nz/groups/profile/935/vln-primary. Through this collective, groups of students from around New Zealand are learning languages together, undertaking project work and sharing teachers.

Through the VLN (Secondary) students are able to participate in lessons using video conferencing. This facility enables schools to share teachers and resources and provide lessons for senior students in subjects not offered at their school. While far from ideal in some instances (there is evidence to suggest many of these lessons are little more than poor replacements for traditional classroom practice), these examples do show the potential for collaboration across schools and the maximising of resources that is made possible (Bolstad & Lin, 2009).

As evidenced in the Global Classroom Project (http://globalclassroom2011-12.wikispaces.com/), the potential for international collaboration between classrooms is enormous. Collaboration can be with any class anywhere in the networked world even in the early childhood years. Their project blog (http://theglobalclassroomproject.wordpress.com/) is evidence of both the ease of collaboration within a project such as this and the breadth of learning possible. Another example of the use of the digital for collaboration is at Concordia College where the senior students collaboratively teach students in the Kalahari in South Africa, using a mix of the digital and face-to-face teaching.

COLLABORATION WITH THE FAMILIES

At the heart of collaborative teaching is involving the students' families more openly and proactively in their learning. As described in Chapter 6, the strongest rationales for implementing collaborative teaching can be found in the benefits for student learning of involving their parents and grandparents more purposefully. Through Web 2.0 tools such as blogs and wikis it is possible to engage with parents in ways never before possible. Some examples from the case studies are provided below.

- At Apiti School, students are videoed demonstrating a new skill; this is uploaded onto their individual blogs where each can show their parents and others what they have learnt. Their speeches are recorded and saved, both as a learning tool for the student who can review past speeches and reflect on what they need to learn, and as a means of showcasing the work to the parents. These examples of student work are linked to their online attainment records where parents can readily access their child's progress against the national standards (password protected).
- At Broulee Public School, one of the special education teachers was taken by the latest special education iPad apps. The apps now offered instructional programs that had previously costs thousands of dollars at a price each family could afford. When coupled with the school's move to BYOT, she could now collaborate with the parents of those students in the astute use of the programs both at home and at school.

The collaboration can be as simple as the regular emails that the principal at Mt Hobson Middle School sends to parents. While there is a weekly email akin to the old newsletter most schools send home (but briefer, more focused on administration), there are also other emails that are not scheduled but sent as required; such as the email updating the status of a child who was injured in an accident, or reminding parents that their child needs to hand in a project that day. The school booklet clearly outlines the roles of the school and the families and how they work together. It also has details on all the projects the students will undertake over the year and the expectations in core learning areas. In addition, the principal often forwards to the parent community literature that underpins the school's vision and philosophy.

Broulee Public School has taken it a step further and has three members of the community (a former director of schools, a former primary school teacher and a graphic artist) providing its parents, grandparents and interested community members with potted advice on what can be done to assist in teaching the attributes that will enhance the young people's success at school. The articles sent weekly by the school in its electronic communication seek to digest the latest research and to translate that language into a form that can be readily understood by all, including those who left school early. That advice is open for all to use at http://web1.broulee-p.schools.nsw.edu.au/groups/mallee/. Significantly, the up-to-date advice supplied to the parents and the school's community has already proved invaluable in the ongoing readying of the teachers.

There are many examples among the case study schools of community members, parents and others who want to support the school and work with them to enhance the learning of students. For example, The Friends' School had a parent come forward to run the school's astronomy group. The school was also asked to accommodate a request from its community rowing coaches to place the training videos on the school web pages for all the students to use. At Balmacewen Intermediate, a parent was used to teach the students about sustainability during a project on wind farms.

CONCLUSION

In the above descriptions of the different approaches we have referred to individual cases as examples, but that is not to say other case study schools are not doing similar things. Nor is it to suggest that this is the only approach being implemented in any one case study school. As will have been obvious, there are natural overlaps between the different approaches. In some instances one example could have sat inside more than one approach.

It is beyond the scope of this work—and perhaps beyond our current knowledge—to clearly describe the complex interweaving of approaches evidenced in these examples. Much work is still to be done on understanding these approaches, on how they are linked and on the benefits they provide. As more schools move to a collaborative approach for teaching and learning, and as interest grows across the educational community, it is likely that there will be increased research and evidence gathered.

However, it is easy to see how once you start on this path, there is a natural evolution and progression to increased collaboration and increased networking and interaction beyond the school. The speed with which this evolution occurs will depend heavily on the leadership of your school, the desire and capacity within the school for change and the extent to which reflection, review and ongoing appraisal is part of your school's culture.

Our sense is that once the school walls are dismantled and collaboration becomes the norm, schools will develop a model of teaching and learning that is multifaceted, flexible and ever-shifting. That is what makes collaborative teaching so exciting.

CHAPTER 5

COLLABORATIVE TEACHING: A VISION FOR THE FUTURE

The vision we have for collaborative teaching is a model of learning that involves all the teachers of young people from birth to school graduation, consciously cooperating and collaborating 24/7/365. It is a model that recognises the importance of a holistic approach that facilitates the enhancement of those attributes—whether academic, thinking, digital, social and/or emotional—that are the key to success at school, in their life and work in the networked world.

It is a vision, we would argue, that has only become possible through the normalisation of the digital and the advent of the networked world. The emergence of increased collaboration in those schools operating in the networked mode is analogous to that provided by the village of old. However, today's is a very different 'village' or community with a strong cyber component. The 'village' that now raises a child is no longer a geographically bound environment; it is a vast world that is both real and virtual. As a result, the number of teachers, the media through which teaching and learning can occur and the resources available to support teaching and learning have never been greater.

We would also argue that the traditional, paper-based and largely insular model of teaching, currently the norm in our schools, has run its course and that it cannot be allowed to continue. Further tinkering within an old paradigm will not dramatically alter outcomes for students; more of the same will not solve the problems of today or those of tomorrow.

Nor is the paper-based model even apposite for the twenty-first century. Something more 'radical' is needed; something more akin to the networked and digital world outside the school gates, the world our young people are currently defining and developing and which they will lead in the future. In this book, we argue that that something is collaborative teaching.

The hope is that collaborative teaching should, in time, be the mode of teaching in all schools, at all levels, in an ever-more networked, collaborative and integrated world. Our vision is of a future where schools will no longer be defined as a set of buildings or as an island in the middle of the rest of a young person's life. Nor will a school's community only be that which is geographically close. Teaching and learning will occur across many different contexts, involve a wide range of players and a growing repertoire of resources.

A DEFINITION OF COLLABORATIVE TEACHING

In defining collaborative teaching, we first considered what *teaching* was. The definition we have used for teaching is that it is any activity intended to bring about intentional learning (Hirst, 1971).

It is then necessary to define *learning*. Again Hirst offers a valid definition, which is that learning is the gaining of a specific achievement, or end state. Learning is evidenced when there is a change in the state of the person who has learnt: they have more knowledge; have greater awareness; are able to do something they could not do before. Their behaviour has changed. Tharp & Gallimore (1991) support these ideas of teaching and learning and describe teaching as 'assisted performance'. They argue that teaching occurs when performance is achieved with assistance.

Understanding these definitions is a critical starting point for understanding collaborative teaching. They are broader than the traditional, formal notions of school-based teaching and learning, although these are definitely included. The notions of teaching and learning, as defined above, can occur anywhere, any time and in any context.

A parent who explains the importance of saying 'thank you' is teaching—the behaviour of their child will change as a result. So is a parent who reads to their child each night—this will improve the child's literacy. The friend who explains an idea is also a teacher, as is the child who uses Google to answer a specific question—both bring about increased knowledge. Note that Google or Wikipedia are not teachers: the child is the teacher when they access the resources—they are the ones performing the intentional act.

We have not included the accidental learning that occurs throughout life—the learning that happens because of other events. The value of experiences, of unintended consequences cannot be discounted, but they are not part of collaborative teaching, except where they are used retrospectively by others to intentionally teach something. For example, the child who breaks something and is made to pay for it has been taught a lesson by the person who made them pay, not by the act of breaking something.

We are not going to discuss whether teaching occurs when nothing has been learnt. For example, the child who does not say 'thank you' has not gained new knowledge; their behaviour has not changed. That is a philosophical question akin to whether a tree really falls if no-one hears it and beyond the scope of this book. Something for consideration though: Whose responsibility is the learning? Teaching has occurred but the child has not been taught …?

The final definition to consider is that of *collaboration*. What does it mean to collaborate? The *Collins English Dictionary* defines the verb 'collaborate' as 'to work with another or others on a joint project'. Regarding collaborative teaching, the joint project is the learning of the individual child; those working together are the child's many teachers who have the potential to play a role in that learning. This is very close to notions of partnerships, which is defined as 'a contractual relationship between two or more persons carrying out a joint business venture with a view to profit'. Translating this latter definition into something more relevant to collaborative teaching suggests that the joint venture is the achievement of our young people; profit is the success that comes when a nation's young people are well-educated, participatory global citizens.

So we can define collaborative teaching as:

when one or more teachers, formal and/or informal, work together with the intentional purpose of enabling or enhancing the learning of a child. Such learning is evidenced by a change in state in that child.

Thus the book title, *Collaboration in learning*.

THE POTENTIAL TEACHERS IN A CHILD'S LIFE

The figure below is a graphic representation of the many different teachers who have a role to play in a child's learning: their parents and grandparents, the community, their professional teachers and other coaches and tutors, their peers and the young people themselves. Sitting behind the collaboration wheel are multiple contexts for learning: the school, the home, the sports field or drama class, the local shopping mall or community centre, and others. Collaborative teaching enables bridges to be built between these contexts or environments, for information, knowledge and learning to be shared across them.

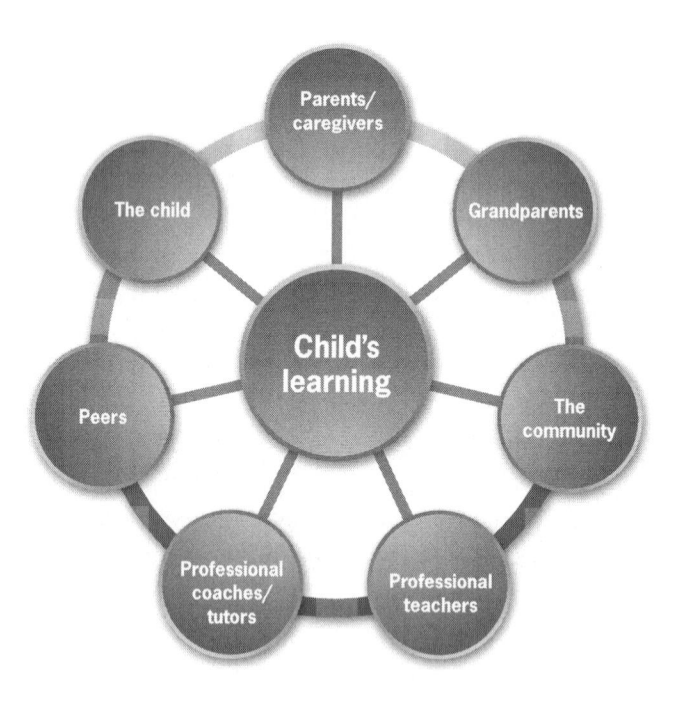

Figure 5.1   The Collaboration in Learning *wheel*

In earlier work, Lorrae has discussed the potential of digital technologies to create richer educational environments for young people (Ward, 2012). This discussion included a detailed explanation of the Zone Theory of Development (Valsiner, 1977) and the two zones within which a child learns: the Zone of Free Movement (ZFM) and the Zone of Promoted Action (ZPA). It was argued that through the use of digital technologies it was possible to connect the many contexts across which a child learns to network their world, thus extending and enriching both their ZFM and their ZPA.

Sufficient for the purpose of this book is the understanding that young people currently participate in what are essentially isolated communities of practice (Wenger, 1998), be it through sport, school, leisure activities or their homes. In the traditional paper-based model, these environments will remain largely unconnected, operating independently of each other. In a networked world they would no longer be unconnected; bridges would have been built. Collaborative teaching is not only about building bridges between those communities, but more importantly about ensuring the teachers within them are working in partnership, not in isolation, for a common purpose related to the development and the learning of the young people.

COLLABORATIVE TEACHING EXPLAINED

In our vision of collaborative teaching (as depicted in Figure 5.1), a child's learning is the hub, the focal point for teaching that occurs across multiple contexts, utilising the expertise of multiple teachers. Key to its success is that all teaching is recognised as an important spoke in the overall wheel. In this model of teaching, it is understood and valued that young people learn at different times, in different places and in different ways; that all teaching and learning contributes to their development.

Collaborative teaching seeks to marry and improve that combined effort. It seeks to link the teaching that occurs across the many contexts of a child's world, including that within the school. It is about each teacher offering a particular skill set, of contributing to a holistic learning outcome. It is not about everyone offering the same skill set and same knowledge.

In suggesting that collaborative teaching is the way of the future, we are not undermining the work of the professional teacher in the classroom. The intensive teaching within the school walls is important, but so too is the teaching that occurs beyond the school gates. We are arguing that there are many other teachers in a young person's life who can and should take responsibility for some of the learning that is needed for young people to reach their potential. We are asserting the importance of the learning that occurs beyond the school gates and outside classrooms walls. To date, the professional teachers, convinced that those in positions of authority in a school somehow know best, have tended to sideline most of those other teachers. In turn, many of those others have been willing, even eager, to leave all the teaching to the professional teachers—to abdicate their responsibility. Implementing collaborative teaching, where everyone works in partnership, will not be easy.

Nor are we talking about an entirely digital world; face time is critical. What we are arguing is that the collaborative and connected norms of the world outside the school should be brought inside; that schools can learn from the world outside and actively embrace the resources available there.

The implementation of collaborative teaching requires you to ask some hard questions about where, when, with whom and how students learn best. It requires you to map the teaching and learning that is necessary for the twenty-first century, attributing responsibility where it is best placed. For example, who is best placed to teach core skills like self-control, human networking or digital literacy? Where are those attributes best taught?

We have yet to unearth any research that fleshes out who should be responsible for what. Instead there seems to be rules of thumb and educational norms that are no longer questioned. Teachers have glibly said particular attributes are the parents' responsibility, and parents have said similar things. Collaborative teaching calls for greater awareness, greater cooperation and more focused partnerships.

SCHOOLING IN A COLLABORATIVE WORLD

We focus in this book on the influence of collaborative teaching on schooling—on what occurs when a child is inside a school. We are concerned with the potential of collaborative teaching to transform schooling, to improve not only outcomes but also the learning experiences of children in school, through an enriched and extended notion of what constitutes teaching and learning. We are asking that schools be receptive to the rich resources outside their school gates and the benefits of inviting that world in.

We are talking about a partnership between schools and their students, families and communities that has as its purpose the enrichment of student learning during their schooling. One cannot help to be impressed by the excitement, the energy and the level of teacher, student, parent, grandparent and community member engagement in the case study schools, and to contrast it to schools where so many of the teachers are tired and cynical and filling in their hours.

We realise that collaborative teaching is a huge step for many schools; that for a long time teaching has occurred behind closed gates and closed doors. Collaboration among teachers and schools is a relatively new concept, let alone collaboration with students, families and the wider community. We are also appreciative of the journey that schools must take and of the necessary investment of time, energy and resources. For that reason we applaud and recognise the steps the case study schools have taken towards a model of collaborative teaching.

THE IMPORTANCE OF THE DIGITAL IN REALISING THE VISION

We envisage the normalised, all-pervasive use of the digital by all in the school's community—and indeed its pre-primary community—playing an ever-greater role in the evolution of collaborative teaching. Pause for a moment and you will appreciate that the case study schools operating in the networked mode are historically among the first that have fully normalised and integrated the digital into their everyday operations. This represents a quite fundamental and historic change in the nature of teaching. While that scenario has been talked about since the 1970s, it is only now, 40 years on, that it has become a reality, even though in only a relatively small percentage of the world's schools.

Mention was made earlier of the newness of collaborative teaching. The same holds with the normalised whole-school community's wide use of the digital. The evolution of the two will continue to go hand in hand with developments within, one impacting the other. The increased understanding and ever-rising expectations of all the teachers of young people will constantly open new opportunities for enhancement, as will the ever-more sophisticated technology—and the increased expectations of young people and their families.

Bear in mind that the young people and all their teachers will never again work with such 'limited' technology as we have today. One has only to reflect for a moment and consider the dramatic impact apps have had upon teaching, both in and out of school. The very real progress in artificial intelligence (as exemplified in Apple's Siri) is going to open doors previously unimagined—providing schools open those doors as the rest of the world outside the school gates has done.

Where for many years the majority of teachers were wary of using the new technology, in the case study schools that is noticeably different. Yes, they are early adopting schools, but the overall teaching and learning environment is prompting early and late adopter teachers to embrace the new and the enhancement in learning it provides.

THE ROLE OF GOVERNMENT AND ITS AUTHORITIES

The very real challenge to our vision of seeing this mode of teaching used as the norm across nations is what has to be a school-initiated move across all schools. Governments can mandate from up high, but it will be to no avail until each school is ready to move and has in place the preconditions discussed in Chapter 7.

Governments, politicians and education authority leaders can, however, recognise the value of the move to collaborative teaching, laud the achievements of the pathfinders, place pressure on the other schools to follow suit, ready the teacher educators, provide advice on what those schools need to do to ready themselves and research the opportunities offered by the more collaborative teaching. Most importantly, they can remove the structural impediments frustrating the schools' move to the collaborative mode.

The evolution of collaborative teaching is to be applauded and it flags the virtually inevitable move, in time, by all to the approach. However, its universal usage could be improved by more conscious recognition and support, and the clearing of the way by those in positions of authority.

CONCLUSION

In summary, collaborative teaching seeks to:
- build on the excellent work being done within the school walls
- enhance the teaching by coupling it with that being done outside the school walls by all the teachers of young people
- improve the quality of the contribution by all those teachers
- more consciously improve the quality of the teaching of the young people from birth onwards in every facet of their lives.

Importantly, collaborative teaching seeks to address both the formal and the informal teaching. It seeks to remove the current strong divide and provide a far more holistic 24/7/365 mode of teaching—a mode that enhances in every young person those academic, thinking, digital, social and emotional skills and attitudes that impact on their success at school and in their life and work in the twenty-first century.

We appreciate that our thoughts are based on the work of a relatively small sample of pathfinding schools from across the developed world. But there is ample—indeed, remarkable—commonality of experiences and complementary research for us to highlight the importance of the development, to roadmap the way forward and to project a vision of what might be possible.

We are not seeking to foretell the future, but rather have sought to identify the educational improvement possible if the natural developments are shaped astutely, like the case study schools have done.

CHAPTER 6

THE EVIDENCE FOR COLLABORATION

It is intriguing and somewhat challenging writing a rationale for a development that appears to be largely a natural consequence of the movement of schools of all types to a networked operational paradigm, of greater collaboration with their homes and community and of building upon the normalised use of the digital by all in the school's community. It is made more intriguing by the fact that the development is so consonant with the general developments in the networked society where greater collaboration and integration is becoming the norm, and the fact that there are so many educational reasons for employing a mode of teaching that is highly collaborative. It is as if one had to wait for the last link to be put in place—that is, all the teachers normalising the use of the digital in their teaching—for schools to be able to join the parents, the students and indeed the rest of society in normalising the use of the digital and experiencing the benefits that flow from that use.

It is interesting to note that the global move by schools to employ a 'bring your own technology' (BYOT) model of school technology resourcing is also in large another consequence of the normalising of the digital use and the greater home–school collaboration (Lee & Levins, 2012).

In advocating that your school adopt a more collaborative mode of teaching you will, in part, be arguing that it is a natural consequence of the school going digital and networked and of the need to shape that development. You will also be contending that the development should be shaped by the substantial research relating to all aspects of the teaching of young people in and outside the school, and that your school ought to take advantage of the opportunities that exist in today's world to assist that teaching.

PARENTS AS TEACHERS

Few today would question the research supporting the imperative of developing the key educational building blocks to an appropriate level in the pre-primary years and the lead teaching role parents must play in those years. The research, moreover, affirms the lead role the parents—and in some instances, grandparents and carers—must play from birth onwards in teaching and nurturing; for example, in:

- language (Hart & Risley, 1999; Strom & Strom, 2010)
- the basics of mathematics
- such key social skills like self-control, self-regulation, patience (Strom & Strom, 2010; Wagaman, 2011)
- the child's emotional development (Weare & Gray, 2003)
- the ability to relate to others, collaborate and work in teams
- creativity (Singer & Singer, 2005)
- children's capacity to contentedly spend time alone (Strom & Strom, 2010)
- the setting of high expectations (Patrikakou, 2004; NCREL, 2011)
- self-reflection, personal evaluation and the ability for young people to increasingly take control of their own learning (Strom & Strom, 2010)
- personal goal setting (Strom & Strom, 2010)
- children's responsible use, maintenance of and fluency with the digital technology.

For years, governments and educators have recognised the prime teaching role parents need to play in stimulating conversation (Strom & Strom, 2010), and of using those conversations to increase the children's vocabulary and, in turn, their facility to read. It is easy to forget that in general terms 95 per cent of a child's working vocabulary will be in place by the age of six (Deacon, 2011).

The traditional focus has been on the reading of books, but in recent years with the relative decline in the printed book and the shift to the digital (Chansanchai, 2011), that reading also includes reading from the screen—something readily done at home, in the car or at the beach. Significantly, the research (Cohn, 2007; Levy, 2009) affirms the parents' recognition of the reading imperative, and while some educators bemoan the abandonment of the printed book, parents have for some time recognised (as did the 2009 PISA results, OECD, 2012) that reading can just as readily be developed—particularly with boys—by reading from the screen. Indeed, the advent of tablets and smart phones means that young people are accessing the digital 24/7/365.

Many parents understood earlier than most educators the importance of their children having internet access and being digital-literate (Lee & Winzenried, 2009). Their recognition has driven parents' ongoing acquisition of the digital since the mid-1990s (ACMA, 2007).

One could continue citing and elaborating upon the research, but the point remains that the vast majority of parents understand their crucial role in their children's success at school, they take their teaching responsibilities seriously and are doing the best for their children— usually with little or no recognition, support or assistance from the professional educators. Historically, developed societies have never had such a well-educated group of parents and, very importantly, never had a parent cohort who have largely normalised the everyday use of the digital in their lives. Educators today are working with digitally empowered parents. The analysis of the 2010 Project Tomorrow survey prompted this telling observation:

> Parents have always been allies and advocates for their children in the traditional school environment. With new digital choices, today's parents are now enabling greater educational opportunities for their children, both in and out of school, and at the same time, empowering a new paradigm for the role of parents in education.
>
> Project Tomorrow, 2011, p. 14

Increasingly, schools will be working with the Net Generation, or what Pew Internet describes as 'Millennial parents' (those born after the mid-1980s), whose normalised use of the digital has already changed the way we live our lives.

> The New Web, in the hands of the technologically savvy and community minded Net generation, has the power to shake up society and topple

> authorities in many walks of life. Schools, universities, stores, businesses, even politics will have to adapt to this generation's style of things, and in my view that will be good. Families will have new challenges, too, as their kids explore the world out there online. Life in other words will change, and many people find change hard.
>
> It is only natural to fear what we don't understand.
>
> Tapscott, 2009, p. 8

We are witnessing the emergence of a potentially powerful electoral force whose educational agenda is akin to that being pursued by the schools working in the networked mode. The key is to recognise that in your parents you have a group of teachers which schools should always have been collaborating with; but today you also have a group that is evermore educated and, vitally, has the digital wherewithal to make it that much simpler to more fully use and enhance their teaching capability.

It is also important to note—and to seek to build upon—the parents' increasing digital empowerment and their growing expectation that the schools will collaborate with them in the teaching of their children, particularly in the use of their children's mobile technology in the classroom (Project Tomorrow, 2011; 2012). It is recognised that with often both parents working, time is a major factor. However, recent research (AIFS, 2007; Cohn, 2007) affirms that even in today's time-short world parents are in general spending more time reading to and teaching their children than 30 to 40 years ago. The lift in the male parent's involvement, particularly over weekends, is especially notable.

Most parents want to collaborate in the teaching, but are currently being shut out. The ease and wisdom of the school collaborating with the parents and using their educative capacity more fully are considerable. Developed societies can ill afford not to better harness and enhance the teaching and digital capacity of its homes.

The authors accept that a segment of parents do not provide, for whatever reason, the requisite teaching in the pre-primary years, and as such their children start school already significantly (and possibly permanently) disadvantaged in key areas of learning (Strom & Strom, 2010). It is a concern. There are, however, few parents who don't want their children to have the best possible education. Many simply lack confidence in their ability to support their children or have been alienated from schooling through their own experiences.

The key (as indicated at different points in the literature; Grant, 2010a; Mackenzie, 2010) is to adopt a 'wealth' rather than a 'deficit' approach. What needs to be remembered is that even today with the grossly underused and underdeveloped parent group,

> the best predictor of academic success in the early years is understood to be the extent of parental involvement in the child's learning (Desforges & Abouchaar, 2003, p. 17; Coleman, 1998, p. 155).
>
> Mackenzie, 2010, p. xi

GRANDPARENTS AS TEACHERS

In recent years, particularly with the many working parents, grandparents have come to play an increasingly greater role in the teaching of pre-primary, primary and early secondary age children. This is especially evident in lower socioeconomic communities. Many young ones spend significant time after school with their grandparent(s) before being collected by a parent (Lee & Hough, 2011). Furthermore, Sparks, commenting on the latest USA census, noted:

> More than one-tenth of American children younger than 18 lived in a household with at least one grandparent at the time of Census interviews conducted in 2009, and the number of children living with grandparents instead of their parents has nearly doubled since 1991, according to a June report by the US Census Bureau. Some 7.8 million children lived with at least one grandparent in the household as of 2009, up from 4.7 million in 1991, a 64% jump, and such children make up a larger share of the population as well.
>
> Moreover, grandparents are—hands down—the most common child-care providers for families after parents, particularly for young children: As of 2005, the most recent data, grandparents cared for 13.8% of preschoolers— more than Head Start, day-care centers, and nursery schools combined.
>
> They also provided care for 12.8% of all school-age children ages 5 to 14. The Census Bureau found the average time children spent in their grandparents' care also increased, from 13 hours a week in 2005 to 14 to 16 hours per week in 2006.
>
> Sparks, 2011

Once again, historically this is the best educated and the most active cohort of grandparents developed nations have known and, with the increasing movement of the 'Baby Boomer' cohort into the ranks, that capability will grow. However, in most developed nations that educational capacity remains unrecognised, unsupported, underdeveloped and largely untapped. This is an educational 'resource' that is committed to the child, invariably has that rare commodity called time, has years of life's experiences to draw upon and would personally benefit from feeling valued by their family, community and nation.

We recognise many of this group, like the parents, will need support and training with their teaching. Further, many will be working from an aged paper-based perspective and generally a much lower level of digital fluency, but what emerges from the case studies, particularly at the primary school level, is their desire to learn, to buy the technology for their grandchild's use and to become more digitally fluent.

The same kind of interest—and untapped and underdeveloped expertise—is increasingly to be found in the nation's seniors or, what might be more aptly termed, its elders. In many cultures the teaching role of the elder is well recognised and harnessed, but in most developed nations little or no use is being made in schooling of the often very considerable expertise and interest of the elders. Crucially, an increasing proportion of these elders, like the grandparents, are highly educated knowledge workers armed with the time to help.

The challenge for schools is not to stereotype this teaching resource and simply slot them into the traditional low-skill roles. One of the case study schools found it had in its community a former senior IBM executive fully capable of leading the robotics group. They also had a former documentary maker well able to extend the budding digital movie makers.

STUDENTS AS THEIR OWN TEACHERS

Interestingly, in the twenty-first century with all that is now known about developing the capability of young people, the educational literature makes surprisingly little mention—except at the tertiary level—of the part young people can and should play in teaching themselves, of the increased facility the digital provides for self-teaching and of young people taking ever-greater control of their own learning (Green & Hannon, 2007). While various writings and research since the 1970s has rightly identified the importance of young people gradually taking greater control over and responsibility for their own teaching and learning, few schools today, even at the upper secondary level, have recognised or sought to capitalise upon the very considerable self-teaching facilities open to their students. As you will be aware, the prevailing mantra is that only professional teachers can teach.

With students being assisted by their normalised use of ever-more sophisticated technology, the situation outside the classroom is very different. As the work of the likes of Tapscott (1998; 2009) Meredyth et al. (1998), Prensky (2006), Green and Hannon (2007) and Gee (2007) reveal, the Net Generation has long taken control of its learning in the everyday world and adopted globally a relevant learning style that is in many ways at odds with the far more linear approach used in most classrooms. Google and the like is their teacher of choice—their one-stop shop for answers.

The analysis of the 2009 Project Tomorrow survey of students in the USA (Project Tomorrow, 2010) spoke of the untethering by young people, and noted:

> *Students envision technology-enabled learning experiences that transcend the classroom walls and are not limited by resource constraints, traditional funding streams, geography, community assets or even teacher knowledge or skills.*
>
> Project Tomorrow, 2010, p. 7

Young people have taught themselves—often with the support of their peers (Green & Hannon, 2007)—how to use the digital world, and in the process have over the last 15-plus years developed a universal set of skills, attitudes and mores (many highly commendable and some 'iffy'), now strongly established attributes that educators will struggle to vary let alone fundamentally change. Like an increasing proportion of their parents, they are digitally empowered. They decide from a very early, pre-primary age what and how they will learn outside the classroom, indeed when and where they will learn and, further, will want a greater say in the nature of that learning in the future (Project Tomorrow, 2010).

As the digital technology becomes ever-more sophisticated, intuitive and all-pervasive, it will increasingly enable young people to teach themselves all manner of skills and concepts—and without any support from educators—to personalise their learning. Ask yourself when you last went to a class to enhance your digital fluency, to research an area of interest, to learn how to use an iPad or an app, and then project that scenario to the young people who are completely at ease with the technology. Watch your three-year-old teach her/himself how to use an iPad or activate Siri and you will appreciate the desirability of factoring self-teaching into the modern teaching mix.

THE BENEFITS OF COLLABORATION

The research already points to the educational benefits derived from adopting a more collaborative and open approach, and cultivating a community and a learning environment where the parents, grandparents and students are made that much more aware of the everyday workings of the school, the educational process and what assists to enhance the students' success at school. However, while pertinent, the research only goes so far. It is research undertaken in a paper-based world and does not address the benefits flowing from collaboration in a digital and networked world, and from schools operating within a networked operational paradigm.

Some of those benefits are already evident, such as the sudden and dramatic shift by schools operating within a networked mode to move to a more collaborative mode of teaching, to evolve a model of teaching suited to a networked world, to pool their digital resources and to adopt a BYOT model of school technology resourcing. Other of the potential benefits such as the shift to a more personalised style of teaching, the facility to bridge the teaching and learning inside and outside the school and to use that bridge to refresh both areas are now on the horizon.

However, we are conscious that these shifts are still in the early stages in the movement of schooling into the networked operational paradigm and that the potential for many other, as yet unidentified, benefits is very considerable.

STUDENT ATTAINMENT AND HOME–SCHOOL COLLABORATION

A major benefit of schools adopting a collaborative teaching model involving the parents, grandparents, carers, community elders and the students themselves is the improvement in student achievement. The research by the likes of Doreen Grant (1989), Desforges and Abouchaar (2003), Patrikakou (2004), Berthelsen and Walker (2008), Berthelsen (2010), Hattie (2009) and Lyndsay Grant (2010a; 2010b) has consistently identified the improvement in academic achievement that comes when parents collaborate with the school and better understand the language of schooling.

What is important to note is that enhancement has come from what might be described as a relatively low level of home–school collaboration. The improvement has come from involvement in school events, attendance at parent teacher nights and the like.

> Reynolds and Clements (2005) reported that school programs that provide support and resources for parent involvement in their children's schooling yield greater and longer-lasting benefits than many efforts that consume a large share of public educational spending, such as smaller class sizes and after-school programs.
>
> Berthelsen & Walker, 2008, p. 40

Further, the early signs within the case studies is that collaborative teaching—and the astute use of the digital—is not only improving academic achievement but is enhancing the students' other skills and attitudes, most notably their social and behavioural development. The case studies report on the impact of collaboration upon improved overall school attendance, enhanced student behaviour, greater student self-control, commitment to their learning and willingness to engage in school-related activities. It should come as no surprise that many key skills and attributes are best developed when the teachers and the home work together in the teaching of that skill, each reinforcing the work of the other, each teaching the attribute in context (Strom & Strom, 2010).

While these developments need to be more fully researched, the findings are logically consistent with the body of research cited above.

When one explores the more open and collaborative mode of teaching in the case studies, be it at Noadswood College, South Forsyth High School, Coal Mountain Elementary School, Apiti School, The Friends' School, Broulee Public School, or any of the others, one soon appreciates that the approach is also simultaneously providing many other, often unintended benefits.

BRING YOUR OWN TECHNOLOGY (BYOT)

As indicated, one of the other developments occurring seemingly naturally when schools move to the networked mode and begin to collaborate with their homes is the willingness of the school and the parents to collaborate in facilitating the young people's use of their own personal mobile technology in the home, on the move and, now vitally, in the classroom. Like that of collaborative teaching, the development itself represents a significant shift—one could say an about-face—on the part of the schools. Up until now, such personal technology generally has been banned and the schools have expressed their insularity by adding significant cyber walls to the school walls. The speed of change to this position parallels the shift to collaborative teaching.

While it is appreciated that there is a body of schools and education authorities moving to introduce a model of BYOT that sees no collaboration with the homes, the expectation is that that approach will soon wither (Lee & Levins, 2012). The key is the collaboration and having the owners of the technology willing to cooperate by taking their personal technology into the classroom. Schools working in the networked mode appreciate that imperative. Interestingly, virtually all of the case study schools have begun a BYOT approach, are planning to do so in the near future or simply allow students to use their own technology when needed.

What is important is that the school's introduction of BYOT markedly assists its collaborative teaching moves and provides each student with the technology needed to assist the personalisation of his or her teaching. With BYOT, the young people have 24/7/365 access to their personal digital office and tools.

THE POTENTIAL FOR PERSONALISED LEARNING

For over half a century, leading educators have striven to enhance student learning by providing each student with a more personalised mode of teaching. From the efforts of the likes of Countesthorpe Community College with its individualised teaching in the 1970s onwards, various efforts have been made to provide a more personalised mode of teaching, but while that desire is still as strong as ever, most teaching still revolves around the class group, albeit seeking to tailor the teaching to the individuals therein.

> *To understand children's personal learning agendas, teachers and parents need to have a deep relationship with children, in which children are able to express their voices and perspectives on their learning experiences. Listening to children's perspectives allows parents and teachers to see beyond the child they would like or expect to see, to the 'third child'. This is the person the child him or herself wants to be, 'the most powerful child, with the most work to do, the agent of his/her own learning'. Fundamentally, this means a commitment to listening to children and seeing them and their learning from their own perspective, rather than seeing them as we would like or expect them to be.*
>
> Grant, 2010a, p. 14

A collaborative model of teaching that actively involves the teacher, the family and the child in each child's teaching, and takes advantage of the support possible with increasingly sophisticated technology, should be able to make significant inroads in better personalising the teaching while also enhancing the child's social and emotional development. Add BYOT, and the school suddenly has the tools it requires to facilitate the personalisation.

BRIDGING THE DIVIDE

Mention was made earlier of the young people of the world using their own style of teaching and learning that grew from the 24/7 use of the digital and online, and making extensive use of social networking, collaboration and self- and peer teaching with little or no call on professional educators. While the approach has been used universally by the Net Generation since the mid-1990s and its impact on the learning of young people and society in general has been profound (Tapscott, 2009), it is rarely acknowledged in education circles.

In brief, the world's young people have evolved a mode of teaching and learning for the digital and networked world. It is not perfect, but there are many aspects which constructivist educators would wholeheartedly endorse.

In contrast, formal schooling continues to struggle to attune its old paper-based approach to accommodate the digital and the networked. Collaborative teaching and the complementary use of BYOT afford an excellent bridge between the two models of teaching and learning, give teachers an invaluable working insight into how the young people teach themselves outside the classroom and provide the opportunity for astute educators to use the knowledge to refresh the school approach.

STREAMLINING AND IMPROVING TEACHING

As suggested earlier, collaborative teaching developed astutely, drawing the best from the teaching both inside and outside the school and making everyday use of the digital, has the facility to become the teaching mode of the networked world and remove to the archives the old separate formal and informal teaching models. However, to do so will entail the ongoing refinement of the collaborative teaching, some serious questioning of what, to many, are givens about the current school teaching, the streamlining of the current teaching undertaken by the home and the school and the ongoing enhancement of the teaching of the non-professional teachers.

What kind of communication or coordination is provided by your school to the home to ensure that a common line is taken on the teaching of key attributes or that there is no unnecessary overlap? Is there any? In most situations it will be non-existent.

One of the important opportunities afforded by collaborative teaching is the facility to openly identify the major teaching responsibilities that should be borne primarily by the home and in turn by the school, and to flag those attributes that the home and the school should teach collaboratively. We couldn't locate any such breakdown by any school or education authority and suspect it might not have been done. We have encountered throwaway lines like 'that is the parent's responsibility' or 'stay out of that, it is the teacher's job', as you probably also have, but never a concerted analysis.

One of the important early tasks in the shift to a more collaborative approach, therefore, could be the compilation of a general analysis, and the identification of the general teaching responsibilities at the different stages of the young person's development from birth onwards. It may well be the analysis that supports in very general terms the present on-the-ground division of responsibilities. Vitally, however, it will provide both the schools and the homes with the facility to more effectively and efficiently focus their efforts, to dovetail their teaching and, importantly, to identify where work is required. It is appreciated that the analysis could generate some warm debates, but in the end it should help both the school's and the parents' teaching and, vitally, enhance the young people's education.

A follow-on to that analysis, which once again has the potential to further enhance student learning, is the vast opportunity to improve the teaching capability of all the teachers of young people—the parents, grandparents, community members and, as flagged, the young people themselves.

We are not recommending insulting parents or grandparents by putting them through 'teacher training' programs; rather, we are suggesting using (like all the case study schools) the potential of the technology and the educational expertise in your school, the school's community and online to readily and inexpensively provide 'just in time' training and support for a grossly underdeveloped teaching resource. As mentioned, not only is the teaching contribution of those outside the classroom not recognised, it is being given scant teaching support.

Professor Susan Deacon, in her review of Scottish early childhood education, made the apt, often forgotten observation:

> ... we need to remember that all of us can support and stimulate the learning and development of a child. You do not need a university degree to encourage a child to play, to stimulate their natural curiosity and creativity or, for that matter, to help out at a local nursery, parents' groups or the like.
>
> Deacon, 2011, p. 17

That holds at all levels of schooling. The support can be provided inexpensively by deploying some face-to-face teaching time to 'teach the teachers', with the kind of face-to-face and online seminars conducted by Noadswood School, or by using senior students as in the case of Concordia College, or interested, well-educated school community members as in the case of Broulee Public School.

From your perspective, what is significant is that all of these initiatives have been mounted by the individual school, using its own resources with scant or no support from the central authority. What bears noting—indeed, underscoring—is that all the case study schools have reached a stage in their evolution where they can see the immense potential in collaborative teaching and recognise they have to assist if that potential is to be realised. All the case study schools recognise they are at the beginning of their collaborative teaching and, most importantly, their leadership is thinking within the networked mode, understands who they need to involve, can envisage the long-term returns on their investment and knows they have to put in the hard work if they are to realise those returns.

CONCLUSION

The kind of collaborative teaching we have in mind is very different from what we have known. But as you reflect on the world around you and what lies ahead, and ponder the sophistication of the skill set your young people will need in that world, we hope you can appreciate why we proclaimed at the outset that this has the potential to be the teaching mode of the networked world.

CHAPTER 7

GETTING READY FOR COLLABORATION

The arguments in favour of the shift to a more collaborative mode of teaching are very powerful. Most have been evident to many educators and public policy developers for decades. Despite this, as indicated earlier, the home and the school have not often or readily collaborated in the teaching of young people. We believe there are two key reasons—one relatively easy to remedy, the other harder. We have taken the stance that the professional educators are the key to successful collaboration; that they must take the lead and actively seek opportunities to collaborate. This is because of the power that currently lies within education for schools to either shut out or include the parents and the community.

Professional educators are the gatekeepers to formal education and often hide behind the idea that the professional knows best regarding teaching and learning. For change in teaching and learning to occur there needs to be a readiness for change—both the capacity and the willingness to change are critical. Teachers and schools need to be able to implement the desired changes *and* want to do so. Therefore, when we talk of readiness, we are talking of the school being ready and able to engage with the wider community, to implement and facilitate collaborative teaching.

It is our belief that the networked age and the plethora of digital tools available mean it is now much easier to implement collaborative teaching (albeit still with some considerable effort). It is true those tools need to be available, schools and their communities need to know how to use them and to want to do so and both the home and the school need access. But the potential is there to collaborate, as never before—and being connected is the norm for most in the wider world.

The desire to change—the willingness of the professional educators to truly collaborate in educational partnerships—is more difficult to realise. We are talking of a fundamental shift in the way teaching and learning is viewed, in the way a number of groups interact and relate to each other. Most significantly, we are talking of a shift in power, away from schools and back to the home and the community. The reality is that we are talking about reframing the role of schools in the teaching of young people. To implement collaborative teaching, much of the 'grammar of schooling' (Tyack & Tobin, 1994) needs to change; the deeply held views about the role of schools, families and communities and the way they work together must be revisited. This must start in the school. The failure of so many reforms to make a difference in the classrooms attests to the importance of the teacher.

The school's principal and its teachers have to perceive the value of the new approach, leave behind the insular outlook, begin dismantling the old school walls, cede some of their educational powers and genuinely respect the contribution made by all the teachers of young people. The wider community also has to be willing to collaborate, accept some responsibility and believe that the schools genuinely want their input.

HOW READY ARE SCHOOLS?

Logic would suggest that in an increasingly networked and integrated world, where so many of the old boundaries and divisions are disappearing and previously disparate operations are being integrated, every school ought to be open to a more collaborative approach to teaching that involves all the teachers of young people.

However, the reality is that at the time of writing the vast majority of schools in the developed world are not willing or ready to collaborate with those other teachers. Indeed, it almost feels as if they are 'drawing the wagons ever tighter'. As calls for accountability and better outcomes for students continue to dominate educational discourse, it seems as if schools are withdrawing behind a defensive line behind the argument that the professionals know best. In a time of increasing accountability, greater collaboration and transparency take courage and the conviction of the value of being part of the wider world.

Whether this will change in two, five or ten years' time we can but surmise. What we do know is that a growing number of schools that have normalised the use of the digital in all classrooms are moving naturally to a more collaborative model. Seemingly overnight, the leadership and teachers of those schools are willing to collaborate with the homes like never before. The collaboration takes many forms: it can be fully face-to-face or wholly online, but in most instances it entails a mix of the face-to-face with the digital.

The case study schools tell us that what they gain from their students participating in a networked and extended learning environment far exceeds any workload or transparency issues; that the 'problems' they face are worth solving. As the principal at Apiti School explained, her students take more pride in their work and put in more effort because they know it will be viewed by a genuine audience: it has a real purpose.

There are other people to consider and to prepare for collaborative teaching for it to be a success, but the first issue is how you win over the relevant educational professionals and convince them to open their doors. Fail to do that and sadly the school will stay with its traditional mode of teaching, largely oblivious to any teaching or learning happening outside the school gates.

The question you have to address at this point is whether your school and, in particular, its leadership and teachers are ready to shift from the traditional insular mode of teaching to one that is more collaborative. Are they ready to cede some power back to the parents and students and to be more transparent about what happens in their classrooms? Are they ready to work with others? Are they of a mind to do so?

THE IMPORTANCE OF THE DIGITAL

Is the normalisation of the digital a precondition to the professional educators collaborating with the students' other teachers? At this point in the journey we don't know, but we strongly suspect that it is. Logic suggests that one should be able to achieve the desired change in the educators' mindset without the digital, but at the time of writing we could find no such instances in all mainstream schooling or in the literature. We would not dismiss the possibility of it happening, particularly as the societal pressure and news of the pathfinders' achievements grow. But at this juncture, what we can say is: achieve whole-school normalisation of the digital and you will have a school staff willing (and indeed desirous) to adopt an ever-more collaborative mode of teaching.

Use of the digital has been a key variable in the case study schools we examined. It has not always been highly visible, but dig beneath the surface and you can see it has been critical. A mindset change seems to occur in both the teachers' and the school's thinking when a critical mass of the teachers in the school (70–80 per cent) normalise the use of the digital in their teaching; perhaps more accurately, when they realise that the digital opens their classrooms to the world like never before—and when they welcome that opening. These teachers quickly recognise the educational worth of working with the home in the teaching of their students, and soon understand the opportunities that the digital and the networked provide to enhance the quality and effectiveness of the learning.

It should be no surprise that in the case study schools the classroom blogs tend to be open to the world, not password protected. The activities of their students are proudly shared with all who are interested. Further, they welcome feedback and interaction from that wider world.

To what extent has your school normalised the digital? The experiences of the pathfinders suggest to us that if your teachers have embraced digital technologies (and in particular are utilising Web 2.0 tools to broaden the learning experiences of their students), then they are very likely to be of a mind for collaborative teaching. If they have not normalised the use of the digital, they are still operating in a silo-like mindset and the shift to the collaborative model will be much greater.

We strongly recommend that you focus on normalisation as the first step towards collaborative teaching; provide the teachers and students with the tools to readily collaborate and then support them to do so. Our sense is that the two go together—that both are about looking beyond the school gates, transcending the classroom walls. Try to implement collaborative teaching and it is likely the digital will need to become normalised. Normalise the use of the digital (and in particular Web 2.0 tools) and increased collaboration is likely to occur naturally over time.

When you have normalised the digital in your school, then the school community will be ready to teach collaboratively—both attitudinally and technically. For this reason, we briefly discuss the normalisation of the digital in this chapter rather than in the next chapter, treating it as one of the preconditions for collaboration focused on learning, for collaborative teaching.

NORMALISING THE DIGITAL IN THE SCHOOL

To achieve normalisation requires the school to simultaneously address the following nine key human and technological variables:
- teacher acceptance
- working with the givens
- teacher training and teacher developmental support
- the nature and availability of the technology
- appropriate content/software
- infrastructure
- finance
- school and education authority leadership
- implementation.

It is not our intention to discuss each of these variables in depth in this book as they relate to digital technologies specifically. That has been done elsewhere in Lee and Winzenried, *The use of instructional technology in schools* (2009). In addition, Mal Lee has summarised and updated these ideas on his blog at http://www.malleehome.com. Of note is the remarkable similarity among many of these and the variables necessary for collaborative teaching to be implemented, as discussed in the next chapter.

However, there are some points regarding the nature of the digital technologies in your school, and who has access and when, that are particularly relevant to being ready for greater collaboration with the world beyond the school.

Historically, teachers have shown a reluctance to move their class to the technology. The tools have to be in the room and able to be seamlessly integrated into the teaching without any loss of time. It is why paper, the pen and the teaching board were universally used. It is why having an interactive whiteboard in each classroom has been the greatest mover of teachers from a paper to a digital teaching base (Lee, 2010).

As a given, every one of your teachers has to be provided with their own digital tools. Every employer should have those tools and have them updated when required. Sadly, today, far too many school employers have still not provided their teachers with that technology. Bear in mind that if the teachers don't have the digital tools to use in their classroom, the students will not experience the use of the digital in those rooms. The tools need to be portable, for personal use and readily connected at both school and home. The teacher laptops (TELA) project in New Zealand has proven the value in providing individual teachers with laptops (Parr & Ward, 2010).

Every teaching room has to have an appropriate mix of whole-class presentation and student-creation digital technology connected to a high-speed network, ready for the teachers to use the instant they desire. It is not enough to have that set up in only some teaching rooms. If your school is still reliant on computer labs, you will have no chance of normalising the whole-school use of the digital. Both teachers and students need ready, instant and flexible access for the ubiquitous use of technologies that signal their normalisation. In brief, if there is not an appropriate suite of digital technology in a classroom, the teachers naturally will continue using the instructional technology that is there—the paper, the pens and the board.

Special mention should also be made of the lead role of the principal in achieving whole-school normalisation of the digital. The principal has to make his/her expectations of all staff, including the casual teachers, abundantly clear in both word and deed (Demski, 2012). In researching the teachers' use of the digital, the authors noted the number of principals who wisely used the teachers' administrative responsibilities to 'prompt' the everyday use of the digital. They astutely used a 'carrot and stick' approach in getting all on board.

If the digital is not normalised in your school, we recommend you refer to the publications mentioned above and others and talk to the pathfinders in this area. There is a substantial literature on the integration of technology into teaching and learning—a good starting point. Much of what you learn there will also have relevance for the implementation of a collaborative model of teaching and learning.

How long it will take to achieve the normalised use of the digital will depend on the situation in each school and a host of variables therein. Suffice it to say the authors have researched schools—particularly primary or elementary schools—that have moved from a paper to a digital base within a year to 18 months. It will be time well spent, given that many of the changes you will be making will also be preparing your school for collaborative teaching.

EQUITABLE ACCESS

In the previous section we talked of the professional educators in your school normalising the digital, of them and their students having ubiquitous access in the classroom. In this section we turn our attention to the need for the students and their families to also have both access and the expertise in order to collaborate with the school in a digital and networked world outside the classroom.

Provision of quality access to the internet is central. In readying the school and students to adopt a more collaborative model of learning that builds on the normalised use of the digital, the authors believe it is imperative that all the students in the school and their families have the appropriate technology and home internet access. Our research has us believe that the individual school should take operational responsibility for looking after the digital needs of each and every one of its students. Limiting access to some students because others do not have it is not an option; finding ways to give everyone access is.

While there is much the local education authority and the national government can do to assist, the onus should be on the school to ensure that relative equity of usage occurs by finding ways to support those who do not have ready home access. This could include allowing for community access to the school infrastructure outside school hours and ensuring that students have access immediately before school, at lunchtime and after school. It could also include talking to the local library or community centre and ensuring they are aware of the needs of your families.

The provision of appropriate broadband access is a responsibility best handled at the national level. It is thus pleasing to note the concerted moves being made in the UK, the USA, New Zealand and Australia to provide all citizens, including their young people, with high-speed internet access and to remove the current blackspots. The national government can also provide financial incentives, such as the tax relief for families of young people in Australia to acquire the requisite technology.

However, there is also much that local education authorities can do to assist. There will be pockets where internet access is still substandard and situations where the young people cannot afford the technology. Those shortcomings should be quantified at the local level and solutions elicited in conjunction with the schools. The local authority knows its context, its socioeconomic mix and the sources it can turn to for support, be it the authority itself, a philanthropic trust, major local companies or indeed service organisations who would be willing to assist those in need.

An early proclamation from the authority about the importance of equity and what it is doing should go a long way to ameliorating many of the community's concerns about a model of teaching that makes everyday use of the digital. The schools can then complement the national and local education authority efforts. The authors' experience in addressing the matter of equity and technology points to the necessity of each school undertaking its own research on each student's situation. All too often equity is used as an excuse for doing nothing.

The naysayers' trump card to any educational development involving technology is often to cite equity, to dismiss the national research showing that almost everyone has access and to say its own community is uniquely disadvantaged—invariably without having put in the hard yards to find out.

With all parties working together, each school should be able to look after its own.

THE READINESS OF THE PROFESSIONAL EDUCATORS

As stated elsewhere, we believe the professional educators are the key to the success of any collaboration, simply because they have the power to close their schools and classrooms, to retreat behind their professionalism. Their readiness to be open and transparent and to work with others is critical.

The principal

The principal has to be of a mind to lead and support the school's move towards greater collaboration. If the principal doesn't see the value and doesn't provide the requisite leadership, the school will struggle. That leadership may be no more than providing the necessary culture for others to take risks and to lead, but the school principal has to empower others to change.

An insight into the leadership capacity required of the principal can quickly be adjudged from their capacity to get a total school staff to normalise the use of the digital. The same attributes are required for both. The research (Lee & Gaffney, 2008; Betcher & Lee, 2009; Lee & Winzenried, 2009) consistently affirms that the movement of a school to the digital phase of its development cannot be achieved without the leadership of an astute principal. If yours has led such a school, the movement towards greater collaboration supporting the learning of your students should be possible. If that normalisation has been achieved at your school, the going should be relatively easy.

If you are the principal, have you empowered your teachers to try new things? Have you asked them to reflect on their current practices? Have you said it is okay to take some risks, or have you focused on keeping things calm, on not making waves? How open is your office to the community? How open are you to new ideas, to different ways of doing things? How aware are you of what is going on elsewhere? Do you know who is in your community and what they can offer your school?

The teachers

As stated already, teachers are the gatekeepers to their classrooms and the students within them. Their acceptance of any change is critical if it is to be implemented. The teachers ultimately decide how they will teach and what instructional technology and resources will be used. Perhaps more critically for greater collaboration, they decide what will be visible to the world outside the classroom and with whom they will interact, when and why. Governments, education authorities and even the best of principals can declare what should occur, but once a teacher closes the classroom door, she/he decides what will happen.

With digital technologies, we know that each teacher needs to perceive the educational benefit of a particular technology or teaching model before they will use it. If teachers believe a particular technology is apposite and its use would enhance the students' learning, they will embrace it. The same is true of collaboration. If they see benefit in opening their classroom, in looking to others to participate in the learning of their students, they will do so. Having said that, in their view the benefits will need to outweigh the effort and time required. Teachers tend to be pragmatics; the practicality ethic runs deep.

To shift your school to a more collaborative and networked model, ideally you will want all teachers of like mind to genuinely collaborate. Think about how open the classrooms in your school are. How comfortable are your teachers about having people wander through while they are teaching? How open are they about what they are doing? Do your teachers have blogs for their classes? If they do, how often are they updated? How much genuine student work is on there—or are they carefully staged and managed showcases?

If your teachers haven't achieved normalisation, the school needs to:
- ascertain the percentage of teachers who are using the digital every day in their teaching
- identify those who are not
- mount a concerted effort, led by the principal, to achieve total normalisation.

If all—or at least the vast majority—have already normalised the use of the digital in their everyday teaching, it is likely the move to the more collaborative approach is already underway, even if only in a small, sporadic way. You will find that the desired mind shift has occurred and the way has been opened for more significant developments. In many ways the hard work has been done.

THE READINESS OF THE OTHER TEACHERS TO COLLABORATE

In our model of collaborative teaching we have highlighted the potential non-professional teachers: the students themselves, their families, their peers, their coaches and tutors, the wider community. Each of these needs to be willing to collaborate, to understand the benefits for both them and the students. Your school cannot take it for granted that they will want to collaborate or will understand the need to do so. For many years parents have been viewed as 'taxi drivers' for their children, as sources of funding and as volunteer workers. They have not often been viewed as educational partners. Similarly, schools have not often involved themselves in the wider community. It could take some time to convince your community that you truly want to collaborate. The extent to which they are ready to do so will vary both across and within these groups.

Do a good 'sales and marketing' job at the outset; have a clear message that is readily understood and give the community confidence that you know what you are doing and why. Also, make it clear that you are together on this journey and that things will change as you learn more about working together; nothing is set in concrete beyond the desire to work collaboratively with the community and the conviction that this will enhance outcomes for the students.

The students

All the indicators point to the vast majority of the students having normalised the use of the digital and to be thinking in networked mode (Green & Hannon, 2007; Ito et al., 2008; Tapscott, 2009). Each will be at different points along a digital competency continuum but, as has been evidenced since the mid-1990s (Tapscott, 2009), all will be very supportive of using a collaborative mode of teaching and learning.

Clay Shirky astutely observed:

> It's when a technology becomes normal, then ubiquitous, and finally so pervasive as to be invisible, that the really profound changes happen, and for young people today, our new social tools have passed normal and are heading to ubiquitous, and invisible is coming.
>
> Shirky, 2008, p. 105

Today, the invisible is nearly here.

The young people will usually not be harbouring the same kind of concerns about collaborating with teachers as many parents and grandparents will. You may well have students who need assistance in securing their own technology, but probably none who do not want to collaborate. They live in the networked world and understand social networking and communication better than anyone.

The parents

The vast majority of your school parents will also have normalised the use of the digital in their lives and work, be attuned to using it as an everyday part of their daily activities and be geared to ensuring they and their children remain abreast of the technological developments. Increasingly, more of them will be Net Generation parents and, as such, will not only be competent in the use of the technology but, vitally, like the young people, will also think networked and will expect (most assuredly, not oppose) the school to adopt the same approach.

As indicated in the Project Tomorrow survey results (2010; 2011; 2012), many parents will naturally expect teachers to use suitable technology in their teaching and that they will collaborate with them to enhance the learning of their children. Moreover, they will expect much of the everyday collaboration to be done digitally.

In making these general comments, be conscious that in the parent group there will be a wide spread of digital competence, with some likely to appreciate appropriate support and advice. The experience of the case study schools would suggest that along the way it would be opportune for the school to get a better understanding of the level of access the students have to the technology in the home, and to build into their strategy advice for parents on how some might more effectively use the internet and of its value as an educational tool.

You can also expect a spread that indicates how ready attitudinally the families of your students will be to collaborate. Many may not have pleasant memories of school or may have been made to feel unwelcome in the past. Gaining their trust and support may not be easy. In general terms, the task should be that much easier at the primary than the secondary level, even though the latter collaboration is still very important, as the research attests (Patrikakou, 2004). As you will well remember, by upper secondary school level most students don't want their parents involved in their schooling—they want to take control of their own teaching and learning.

When commenting on Noadswood School's Year 7–12 efforts to teach collaboratively with the parents from Portsmouth in the UK, Dr Tim Ennion spoke of the enormity of the challenge of changing the parents' perception about collaborating with the teachers at the secondary level, but particularly in the senior years. The principal at Apiti School described the difficulties she was experiencing in getting support from some parents who did not see value in what the school was doing. Talking to these parents, taking every opportunity to educate them and to respond to their concerns is critical.

The grandparents

The case study school experience mirrors that of the research mentioned earlier that reveals in many situations, particularly at the primary school level, that grandparents are playing a significant role in the teaching of their grandchildren, especially in that key learning time immediately after school and until the parents return from work. The case studies indicate that most grandparents are very conscious of the importance of providing the young people access to the digital and guiding its wise use, but many openly admit to their lack of digital competence or even awareness.

The socioeconomic profile of your school's community could impact on the proportion of your grandparents' and indeed carers' and community elders' readiness to use the digital, and thus it bears remembering in your implementation. Moreover, not surprisingly, most still use the traditional paper-based frame of reference. That said, most are highly committed to supporting their grandchildren, are keen and have the time to collaborate and, within examples from the case study schools, often constitute a significant portion of the online and face-to-face seminars run by the school.

In your planning of any face-to-face or online seminars for parents, simultaneously open the doors to interested grandparents and community members—and in particular its elders. You, like the pathfinders, might find that by partnering with groups like the U3A (University of the Third Age) and senior computer user associations, much of the training will be handled by them.

CONCLUSION

The simple point we wanted to make in this chapter is that careful thought needs to be given to your school's readiness to embrace a more collaborative model. The key may well lie in the extent to which the digital has been normalised. This will give you a sense of the readiness of your school leaders and teachers to move beyond the traditional paper-based and silo-like school model.

As you've read the above and reflected on the situation in your school, some of you will recognise that your school has already begun the shift naturally, while others will appreciate the enormity of the work to be undertaken before the school can even contemplate suggesting such a shift. While restating the obvious, every school's situation is different, even within the most centralised of education authorities and, as such, you have to ascertain your school's readiness to embrace greater collaboration with those outside the school gates before contemplating proceeding with any implementation plan.

CHAPTER 8

PUTTING COLLABORATION INTO PRACTICE

If you have decided that collaboration is part of the vision for your school, this chapter is designed to help you achieve your goals. Assuming that the professional educators in your school are both able and willing to collaborate with others and that you have ascertained the capacity and willingness of your community, what are the next steps? If, on the other hand, they are not yet at that stage, you will need to build the development of that readiness into your strategy and implementation planning.

As all the case studies attest, while the school has to genuinely collaborate with and listen to its community, the reality is that the educational professionals have to take prime responsibility for interpreting its community's desires and translating those wishes into the apposite teaching and learning. It also has to take responsibility for describing the proposed shift, explaining the rationale for making the change and mapping out the first steps. In an ever-evolving, rapidly changing twenty-first century, as Steve Jobs and Apple so brilliantly identified (Isaacson, 2011), it is not good enough to rely solely on focus groups to identify the best way forward: the professionals have to provide an educational experience that the clients will embrace but might yet be unable to articulate.

Like a pathfinder, he [Jobs] could absorb information, sniff the winds, and sense what lay ahead.

Isaacson, 2011, p. 566

You will need to develop a clear vision and a strategy for moving forward that is accessible to the wider community and clearly outlines the benefits for all concerned along with their roles and responsibilities in the early stages. The school leadership will need to be ready and willing to answer questions, to listen carefully and to be flexible. The challenge for school leaders (like that for the technology leaders) is that they will be planning for a journey into a world they don't as yet know and where few have travelled. Fortunately, as evidenced in the stewardship of the case studies, there are many wider society and industry cues to help shape and guide the journey, not least of which is the importance of factoring into the planning the ready facility to change course if the need arises.

THE STRATEGY

Your implementation strategy needs to be one suitable for a school working within a networked operational paradigm where the organisation is constantly changing and evolving, where one needs to primarily shape and manage, and where you will be moving into uncharted territory. It needs to take into account the current state of readiness across your community (as discussed in the previous chapter) and work from that point. Every school will be at a different place and have different areas that need focusing on before they can move forward.

Unashamedly adopt a big-picture development strategy—consistent with the school's shaping educational vision—that provides you with the ready flexibility to vary the school's approach as you move through the unknown. The traditional three- or five-year strategic plan that identified what you were to achieve at key dates was designed for an era of constancy and continuity. When one is challenged today to read the scene six months ahead, such an approach can be meaningless. That said, virtually all the case study schools had to satisfy the demands of their local bureaucracy by submitting such a plan that kept the bureaucrats happy but made little contribution to the school's development.

Think networked and collaboration

In the shaping of your strategy, think networked, abandon the unnecessary constraints of the old school walls and seek to provide a mode of teaching and learning that can occur anywhere, any time, 24/7/365. Fundamental to that approach is genuine collaboration among all the teachers of young people and those supporting that move and, vitally, a genuine respect for and support of the contribution all are making.

You are likely to recognise early that your understanding of the concept of collaboration is relatively simplistic and will need ongoing development. The reality is that one cannot expect to move from years of shutting all but the education professionals out of the teaching and learning process and overnight employ a highly sophisticated model of collaboration akin to that employed in many industries. A key facet of the implementation strategy, therefore, ought to be an ongoing refinement of the understanding of collaboration by all within the school's community. This includes a recognition of when—and when not—to use the approach and the gradual adoption of ready-to-use metrics, such as those proposed by Hansen (2009), that enable the school community to adjudge the effectiveness of the collaboration.

A shaping educational vision

Naturally your strategy has to be consonant with the school's evolving educational vision and its overall development strategy. Your vision needs to be one that will shape your school's future.

That said, a number of the case study schools soon recognised that their supposed shaping vision was too 'wishy-washy'—too much a 'motherhood' kind of statement. It did not provide the school with any real direction and most assuredly did not help the decision makers identify whether a proposed initiative was consistent with the school's objectives. One of the principals interviewed believed her school's vision was more appropriate for a retirement home!

Supporting the shaping vision needs be a succinct, easy-to-understand explanation of why the shift to greater collaboration, why you are looking beyond the school for support in enhancing student learning, what the benefits are for all concerned and how they will be realised. Your vision statement should be in a style that every parent and grandparent—including those who left school early or became alienated with schooling—can understand. They should be able to see 'what is in it for them' and where they fit.

The importance of the vision statement relates to the early comment about a big-picture strategy.
- Does your existing shaping vision do the job?

- Does the wording you are using identify the desired big picture and support the moves to a more collaborative mode of teaching?
- Is it readily understandable and meaningful across the whole school community? Can everyone 'see' themselves in it and what it means for them?

Remember:
- Write your vision and supporting statements for all your community, not just your teachers.
- Make sure everyone is included.
- You definitely don't want 'psychobabble'. Have clear and powerful statements that can be used on the school's website and in its publications.

MAKING COLLABORATION A REALITY

Once you have developed your guiding strategic documents, you need to consider the implementation in more detail. There are a number of things you need to think through at the outset, which are discussed in the sections below. Remember there is no one answer; much depends on your current position. Also remember that flexibility and the willingness to alter direction are going to be critical to long-term success.

Natural evolution or a planned move?

One of the vital lessons to emerge from the case studies is the importance of letting the natural shift to greater collaboration grow and evolve of its own volition. The lesson is not to over-plan once your school has normalised the digital and shown a willingness to collaborate. Give the development time to find its own form and take its own course.

We appreciate that this kind of approach is alien to the training most educational leaders are provided (and may horrify the bureaucrats!). However, while it was possible in an era of constancy and continuity to plan almost every development because the end form was known, it is a meaningless exercise when the end form is unknown.

The importance of letting the development grow naturally and gradually take its own form is already well evidenced in another development that has followed a similar path and grown naturally from the normalised use of the digital: the move by schools and education authorities to use a model of BYOT, where the students bring their own technology into the classroom. Forsyth County in the USA, one of the global leaders in the use of BYOT, never planned to move along that route. The development flowed naturally from its teachers' normalised use of the digital and its collaboration with its homes (Lee & Levins, 2012). Talk to the leaders of Coal Mountain Elementary School and South Forsyth High School or St Mary Star of the Sea in Australia and you'll appreciate all are letting the development evolve, are monitoring its growth and will give it an occasional nudge if it is moving too far off course. But all have recognised the imperative of not committing too much to paper until the development clarifies its form. This is a very different development strategy to the traditional and one you are likely to have trouble explaining to the powers on high. But don't let that stop you.

The same kind of approach needs to be taken with the development of collaborative teaching. As indicated earlier, while we have a vision this mode of teaching might take, ours is but a supposition and it is likely that educational outcomes will emerge that were unanticipated and unintended. That is the way of the networked world—and networked school communities.

What hit home with the case studies was not only the many similarities (which we identified in Chapters 3 and 4), but also the diversity of the approaches that have been adopted. Let them emerge. Foster their growth and the diversity—and importantly, try not to over-plan. That said, in all your planning and implementation, integrate the new into the school's overall development plan and ensure it meshes seamlessly with all the other developments.

The nature of the collaboration

While the research discussed in Chapter 6 provides a strong guide early on, you will need to decide what you particularly want to collaborate on, and with whom.

Consistent with the research, it is noteworthy that the case study schools (both primary and secondary) have chosen to collaborate with the parents primarily in the joint teaching of the thinking, digital, social and emotional skills and attitudes and to leave, in general terms, the teaching of most of the academic skills to the professional teachers.

That said, as always, there are some notable exceptions. The most obvious one is the development of literacy from birth onwards and the parents' continued significant teaching role once their children are in primary school. Another is the teaching of what might be termed digital fluency, where there is a growing recognition that the young people's 24/7/365 use of the digital ought to be accompanied by a more holistic teaching of its astute use (Grant, 2010b). That need grows when the local legislature or education authority places major impediments on the use of the students' own technology in the classroom.

It is interesting to note in the case studies how well an inquiry-based curriculum (or what some refer to as a project-based curriculum) provides the opportunity for the school, the students and the parents to collaborate in the teaching of many of the social, digital and thinking skills. In some instances, as at Mt Hobson Middle School, this takes the form of independent learning with increasing responsibility devolved to the students for project completion.

Virtually all of the case study schools are making use of grandparents, community elders or other community experts in the teaching of specialist or extension skills that the school could not normally supply; areas like astronomy, specialist movie making and robotics. Bringing in actors to discuss drama or using circus performers to teach physical skills are further examples of the imaginative ways in which the case study schools utilise the expertise in the community to enrich and enhance their students' learning experiences.

In time, with a better appreciation of each other's capabilities and who is best placed to teach what and where, there would be considerable benefit in mapping out in general terms who has responsibility for teaching each of the key educational building blocks at key stages in our young people's development.

Support and training

The provision or readying of the development and support materials that will enhance the teaching by all (the professionals, parents, grandparents, community members and students) should be an important component of the initial and ongoing enhancement of your teachers, both in and outside the school. If, for example, the plan is to make extensive use of class blogs and wikis, every teacher—including the regularly employed casual teachers—need to be readied to use them to the best advantage.

- What plans do you have for the students?
- If the intention is to enhance the parents' and grandparents' understanding and use of metacognition, how is it to be addressed?
- What kind of support and training are you providing your parents?

For example, look at the online resources of Noadswood School in the UK: http://www.noadswood.co.uk. Broulee Public School in Australia, through its digital communications suite, provides parents with a weekly digest of the latest research on the factors impacting on the students' success at school: http://web1.broulee-p.schools.nsw.edu.au/groups/mallee/. Others, such as Apiti and Pukeokahu schools in New Zealand, have worked with their parent communities offering digital technology courses to better enable them to access the materials available on the school's wikis.

What is already apparent with all the case study schools is that they all appreciate that they have barely scratched the surface in this area, are only now beginning to understand how best to provide the support and development for each type of teacher and the very real but vital challenge they need to tackle. Significantly, with the notable exception of the Forsyth County, all the support and training are being prepared and provided by members of the school's community, be it the teachers or (as with the Broulee Public School example) members of the school's community. In an ideal scenario, conscious that much of the material is generic in nature, the local education authority should provide significant support. The desire to support, rather than control, the schools (as is evidenced in Forsyth County) is an ideal that other authorities ought to consider.

Graduated or all in?

One of the key strategic decisions you will need to make early on is whether to go with a graduated, controlled and measured pilot model or an 'all in at once' approach. Writing in 2009, Lee and Finger (2010) strongly advocated using pilots in the shift to a networked mode. Peter Drucker, the great management guru, noted:

> Neither studies nor market research nor computer modelling are a substitute for the test of reality. Everything improved or new needs therefore first to be tested on a small scale, that is it needs to be PILOTED.
>
> Drucker, 2001, p. 87

Significantly, all the case study schools have on the other hand chosen the 'all in' approach. In 2009, the natural flow-on to a mode of collaborative teaching was still too embryonic to be identified with certainty. Armed with the new awareness and the recognition that the move to a more collaborative approach will be happening in all grades, our suggestion is to follow the case study schools and opt to go with the 'all in' approach.

That said, your approach ought to be strongly influenced by your size and context, and as such needs to be your school's call.

Launch or quiet introduction?

Do you employ a high-profile launch of the school's intentions to collaborate more purposefully and broadly on a specified date, or do you naturally build on existing developments and quietly up the profile? Again, it has to be your call.

Two important factors to consider will be the degree to which the concept is accepted within your parent community and the local political scene. However, in light of the number of the observations made earlier about the need for the school leadership to make the school's intention re collaborative teaching clear to all, the authors suggest there is much to be gained from having all within the school's community understand the magnitude and implications flowing from a move towards greater collaboration.

That can be assisted by a high-profile launch. But there are risks involved: many will be quick to question and criticise, and a high-profile launch can lead to high expectations of quick results.

Promotion

Regardless of what you decide to do with the launch, you will need to constantly and naturally weave the 'selling' of the concept of collaborative teaching through all you do. It will be different and, as such, alien to many in your community, and initially it might be difficult for some to accept. Thus in all you do, you will need to explain the reasons for the new approach. It will be particularly important to sell the concept to new teachers and new enrolments. Remember to focus on the benefits for all.

The case study experience indicates that the approach will start selling itself very quickly if implemented astutely. The students' enthusiasm, the parents' talk around the school grounds and the teachers' pride in the education provided will soon have an impact.

There is also much to be gained by having the approach featured in the local media, educational journals, online forums and the talks given by senior educators and politicians. It is interesting, however, to note those among the case study schools that have naturally increased their collaboration with the outside world and have opted to let it settle in before publicising the move in the media.

Technology

Considerable mention has already been made of the all-pervasive use of the digital, but there are several key aspects that warrant close attention in your planning.

BYOT

Potentially, the most important is what you decide to do in relation to BYOT. As indicated, it too is a natural flow-on from having normalised the whole-school use of the digital. Further, it is another way of collaborating with the homes.

In examining the case studies, it was apparent that all the schools and Forsyth County had moved some way to adopting the model: some had formally done so; others were about to do so; others may have done so without really thinking about it. Our belief is that the two developments go naturally hand in hand, with both working to support the other. However, you need to make the decision based on your situation.

The suggestion is that you read the companion work Lee and Levins have prepared on BYOT (Bring your own technology, 2012), its inevitability, the plethora of opportunities it provides and how one might best introduce the model.

Infrastructure

Allied to (but, if you decide, separate from) the introduction of BYOT is the importance of recognising that the shift to greater collaboration and the very likely increase in the use of the digital by all will require some fundamental rethink of the configuration and form of the school's network.

In brief, you will invariably be moving from a strongly insular model where the operations took place behind the school walls that only a few could breach to an open operation with greater demands and expectations on your network. Many of the case study schools have opted, for example, to use open-class blogs and wikis, which any in the networked world can access.

You will want a network infrastructure that can support and enhance your desired collaboration and the resultant teaching and learning. A vital part of that infrastructure that is likely to be an ongoing challenge as the usage, and hence the traffic, grows will be the level of bandwidth the school has to purchase. It will be an ongoing major cost. Belonging to 'loops' of schools where costs are aggregated and shared is an example of cost-saving collaboration.

Digital communications suite

This is a key facility that is to be found in different forms in all the case studies. Your school will need an integrated multifaceted, multi-way suite of digital communication and collaboration facilities that allow the school to seamlessly, inexpensively and efficiently liaise with all its members and the wider networked world. That is not necessarily as complex—or expensive—as it sounds. Think about what is readily in use outside schools and use that.

The actual form of the suite will vary with the school size and the finances available, but it will invariably include an integrating website, blogs, wikis, possibly RSS feeds, Twitter and Facebook access, email communication with every parent and interested grandparents, carers, community members and organisations, and regular interactive multimedia communication with those interested in the school's operations. Dependence on paper-based communication is not good enough. The key is to have the facility for all those likely to be involved in the learning of your students to readily liaise and communicate digitally. It is a facility you need to have in place before you embark in a significant way on a journey towards collaborative teaching.

Allied to the setting up of the digital communications suite is the need to ensure that the school is ready to run such an operation. For example, the school should have every parent's current email address and the ready facility for any who are desirous of joining the school's digital community to do so. Decisions should also have been made around who will moderate comments made in, for example, blogs and wikis. Most importantly, the permission of all parents to publish their children's photos, work and names online should be obtained.

Again, none of this is as complex or as difficult as it seems. Learn from the world outside, talk to the students, their parents and others. Learn from what other schools and organisations have done.

Synergy

As you do your homework and make ever-greater use of the digital in the teaching, administration, communication, support and training, and eliciting suggestions and feedback, you will come to appreciate the many economies and efficiencies that can come from its astute use and the ever-tighter integration of operations in and outside the school.

You will be able to achieve synergies that were impossible to achieve in a paper-based operation. For example, if your school was to normalise the everyday use of open (that is, not password protected) blogs and wikis in every class, not only could the school facilitate greater collaboration, but simultaneously it could also provide the following:

- an insight into the school's daily activities to parents, grandparents, the local community and the students, and what they can do to complement that work
- advice to parents on the school's program, its calendar of events and the home study
- a window into the workings of the school to all interested professionals, school or system executives or politicians
- an important indicator as to where the school is at in its evolution
- instant, ongoing accountability
- the facility for instant teacher 'evaluation' and an insight into who is adding value
- very powerful marketing of the school
- an appreciation of how well the school operations are integrated.

Importantly, all this can be done as a normal part of the everyday teaching without adding to the teachers' workload and that of the home or the cost.

Refinement and evolution

Only when you begin to collaborate more with those outside your school, will you begin to appreciate the room for improvement and how that might best be done. With the best of intentions, you will start with only a rudimentary networked mindset. While the authors have been researching and analysing collaborative teaching, we have regularly found new opportunities and the necessity of refining our thinking. As we dig deeper, we are continuously amazed at what is happening beneath the radar and without fanfare. After years of constancy and continuity, and knowing what was involved in the running of a good school, it is very revealing and (for us, at least) exciting to work in a context of ongoing and often uncertain and rapid change and evolution, with a completely new group of teachers and within a fundamentally different operational mode.

You will undoubtedly find (like we did) many chances to refine and enhance the ways in which your school is collaborating with others. The key (as flagged above and elaborated on in the next chapter) is to have a development strategy flexible enough to accommodate that evolution, and with the in-built obligation to regularly collaborate with the full set of teachers on how best to enhance not just their teaching but also the learning of our young people.

Measuring achievements

It will be important to consider from the outset how you intend to 'measure' the success of both the shift to greater collaboration and, importantly, its impact on the school, its community, students' attitude and their learning and success at school. What readily understood performance indicators should you use?

We explore the possibilities more fully in Chapter 10. But as you prepare for implementation, contemplate how the school should best measure its achievements.

Authority-wide introduction

We made it clear from the outset that the focus of this book was the move to greater collaboration at the individual school level. We have also stressed throughout that the way forward will be different in every situation. Notwithstanding, it is important to spend a few minutes addressing the issue of how collaborative teaching can be employed across all schools within an education authority.

The answer is most assuredly not the traditional mandate from up high and employment of a 'one size fits all' strategy. It is actually very simple and is neatly exemplified in the work of the central office leadership at Forsyth County. Authorities need to assist each school to normalise the use of the digital in their everyday teaching, remove any unnecessary structural and logistical impediments and, as an authority, publically endorse and celebrate the achievements of the pathfinders while assisting the remaining schools in making the move.

Much of the advice we have already discussed can be used by an astute and tightly integrated central office team to assist all the schools. The key is for that team to act as facilitator and supporter conscious of the different situation in each school, willing to let each school and its community 'grow' its own forms of collaboration.

Once there is any sense of control over the move, that 'we are from the office and thus we are the experts here to tell you what to do', the authority's facility to assist is shot. The central office team at Forsyth County, for example, used bus tours that physically took interested teachers to the pathfinding schools as part of its facilitation and support. It also ensured like-minded schools constantly networked and refined their approach, and were able to sell the notion that each school didn't have to reinvent the wheel. Importantly, while not taking the glory away from the individual schools, the District office acts primarily as the front office for the wider national and international community.

CONCLUSION

At some point—possibly even now after working your way through what might seem to be an extensive To Do list—you might feel the challenge of collaborative teaching is just too great. But when you look at the potential benefits, the way in which society is daily inclining to a flatter, more integrated and collaborative world, and you note the great progress being made by the likes of the case study schools and appreciate all have had to overcome similar if indeed not greater hurdles, it is hoped you will be motivated to continue pushing forward.

Even in their traditional insular form, schools are highly complex human organisations. Add to that mix a very sizeable body of additional teaching resources that need to be seamlessly integrated into the everyday operations of the school, and you have an even more complex, but also immensely richer and more powerful teaching organisation that will require astute leadership, ongoing refinement and an appropriate implementation strategy. As the case study school leaders attest, it will be worth the effort.

CHAPTER 9

AN EVER-EVOLVING DEVELOPMENT

The minute you begin to embrace greater collaboration as part of your school vision, you will embark—knowingly or unwittingly—on a path of ongoing evolution and refinement. In theory, that might have been true in the better schools and classrooms even within the traditional paper-based teaching paradigm; in reality, the constancy and continuity that characterised that mode of schooling also characterised the teaching.

On reflection, there has been no fundamental change in teaching over the last 50 years while schools operated within the paper-based mode. Solitary teachers, working in a classroom behind the walls of a physical place called school, have done the vast majority of the teaching. Occasionally some teachers have team-taught, personalised their teaching, worked with aides, collaborated or taken their class outside the school walls, but in the main teachers have taught alone in front of a massed group called a class within a specified room with minimal liaison with the home.

When schools go digital and, in turn, networked and move to a more transparent and collaborative form of teaching, they irrevocably leave behind the constancy and continuity of old and move to a mode of schooling that will be ever-evolving and ever-changing. In the same way we have seen the working practices of banks, travel agents and surgeons change when they went digital, so too will it change with schooling when it becomes digitally based and collaborative.

The moment when your school begins to contemplate a move to collaborative teaching, it needs to be ready (at least attitudinally) to move astutely with the ever-evolving scene. It has to continually shape the desired teaching. More than ever you will need to be proactive, understand the megatrends and take advantage of them. Sit back and react, and you'll be swamped and your students will be short-changed.

BUT AT THE BEGINNING

While the (obvious) point has already been made, it is important to appreciate that while the collaborative teaching approach is a dramatic change from the past, all the examples of collaboration featured in the case studies are but beginning efforts. Ask any of the case studies and you will find them already contemplating the many improvements they can make. Indeed, one of the principals interviewed felt despondent about how much the school had yet to do, forgetting that she was now thinking within the networked mode, very much aware of the as yet unharnessed potential.

EDUCATIONAL FOCUS

Significantly, all the schools studied—be it the smaller primary schools like Apiti or Pukeokahu schools or the larger secondary schools like The Friends' School and Concordia College and Noadswood School—had as their prime focus the improvement of the teaching and learning of every student and, importantly, the holistic education of those students. There was a strong recognition by all that their collaborative efforts needed to be directed at the 24/7/365 teaching of young people and the enhancement of the total suite of skills needed to succeed in and outside school.

While the secondary schools were highly conscious of the imperative of the A levels or tertiary entrance and the school maximising the students' attainments, each was simultaneously seeking to collaborate in the teaching of the key holistic attributes. For example, in its teaching of senior maths, Concordia College has opted for a more personalised mode of teaching that requires each student to take far greater responsibility for their own learning, while at the same time strengthening in each their capacity to reflect on and evaluate their own performance.

The facility to teach multiple attributes through the one learning task is an important one that should be factored into the ongoing refinement of any collaborative approach. That integration is clearly assisted by the normalised use of the digital.

That said, as you look to the ongoing improvement, be very clear of the learning outcomes you are wanting, as they relate to both the students' performance in the formal 'testing' and those outcomes for long-term success. In identifying and in particular observing the outcomes, be aware of the unintended learning outcomes that might emerge, particularly at this stage of collaborative teaching. A number of those unintended outcomes could relate to the students' wiser use of the technology, their digital fluency, recognising the context to use different types of communication and social skills, their personal organisation and planning and their facility to accommodate rapid and uncertain change.

Celebrate these and recognise their importance. It is simply impossible to foretell all the outcomes that will flow from a new, more collaborative approach.

NETWORKED MINDSET

We appreciate that significant mention has already been made of the desirability of teachers adopting a networked mindset. However, it bears emphasising that it will be the strengthening of that capability that will be one of the main drivers of the ongoing evolution and refinement of collaborative teaching as it is implemented in your school.

What is mainly holding us back is the human mindset, not so much the technology. We all naturally default to the traditional approach. It will take time and generations experiencing greater collaboration for all to think networked naturally and to realise its full potential.

However, if introduced astutely, within a year increased collaboration can bring some significant changes in the staff's thinking. For example, ten months after the launch of its collaborative approach, one of the case study schools evidenced a significant shift. The day after the first performances by its community member-run choir and its concert band, four staff members informed the principal that they were either willing to sit in with the fledgling concert band or assist in its conducting, or would like to approach folk in the community who could help in the teaching of the instruments. As a staff, those teachers had embraced in general terms at least the collaborative approach, working with a mindset that prompted them immediately to ask what resources they had within their community that could assist.

DISMANTLING THE SCHOOL WALLS

Part of the evolutionary process will undoubtedly involve the wider school community increasingly asking why certain types of learning have to be restricted to within the school walls and which of the current internal and external school walls might metaphorically be dismantled. That need will grow as the school's digital communications suite becomes ever-more sophisticated and as more parents, students and politicians come to appreciate that young people don't always have to be physically present at a place to learn (Lipnack & Stamps, 1994).

The learning of digital literacy is one such example, recently examined by Futurelab (Grant, 2010b). You, like us, have to question the rationale that sees personal digital literacy being taught to class groups in schools that ban the use of that personal technology in the classroom and try to do so using networks where much of the likely internet access is severely limited! As Grant (2010b) notes, this is an excellent example of where the skill could far more effectively be taught collaboratively using the young people's personal technology in the real world, free of the constraining school walls.

You are likely to quickly identify many other attributes and areas of learning that should be taught unbounded by the physical school walls. The authors appreciate that for some time yet the constraints required when students are within the physical school may well be necessarily different to those outside its grounds but, notwithstanding, most of you will find many of the current barriers imposed can be safely removed.

EMPOWERING ALL YOUR TEACHERS

Another significant area for refinement and evolution that links closely to providing a holistic, 24/7/365 education and enhancing networked thinking, relates to the fuller empowering of all your teachers. In the traditional pyramid-like organisational structure that still characterises most schools, only the very small group of staff at the apex have the opportunity to view the total workings of the school and to develop the vital macro understanding required to run a complex, tightly integrated school.

In keeping with the traditional factory model, the vast majority of teachers understand only their particular area of responsibility and as such have a restricted view of schooling ill-equipped to make any significant contribution to the overall workings of the school. Maths teachers or drama teachers believe schooling ought to revolve around the teaching of mathematics or drama, and so on. In brief, most teachers, particularly at the secondary level, have been disempowered and their professionalism has remained underdeveloped.

In ever-flatter networked organisations that are beginning to dismantle the old walls and become more tightly integrated, it is vital that all the professional teachers are duly empowered and able to contribute to the shaping of the desired holistic teaching and schooling. It will take time and support to achieve. So, too, will the empowerment of the parents, the grandparents, the young people and the community.

We realise that most schools aren't even aware of how much they have disempowered most teachers, let alone would contemplate empowering the other teachers of young people. When schools embark on the path of greater collaboration what is reassuring is that the thinking changes and everyone better appreciates the importance of empowering all teachers of the young people, including the young people themselves.

THE LEAD ROLE OF PROFESSIONAL TEACHERS

What is also evident—and natural—is that the good professional teachers by dint of their teaching prowess will (and should) play a lead role in the continuing evolution of collaborative teaching. They have the time, the expertise and the commitment. For some, their 'control over' approach will need to be moderated to that of a mentor, facilitator, guide and 'teacher of teachers', but all should be expected to play a lead role.

The 'teacher as teacher' concept is potentially a very important one in the move to an ever-more collaborative approach to learning. Traditionally, teachers have been used in face-to-face teaching and learning situations; of recent times, more are also teaching online. However, as the Virtual Learning Network experience in New Zealand shows, even this is not an easy shift for teachers to make.

When one is desirous of providing greater support and assistance to the teaching of hundreds of parents and grandparents, it makes sense to use some of your teachers to 'teach' the non-professional teachers. As mentioned, some of the case study primary schools in regional areas, well away from the big city support, are already using this approach particularly in the pre-primary and early childhood years. It is a role well worth considering.

THE IMPACT OF NORMALISED SUPPORT AND TRAINING

As indicated in Chapter 8, from the outset your school ought to put in place a concerted program of support for all the teachers of the young people. One would hope that such programs, coupled with the likes of a 'teach the teachers' initiative, would gradually begin to impact on and facilitate the evolution of the teaching provided.

Interestingly, the case study school experience strongly suggests that the support and advisory programs mounted for the non-professionals unwittingly also works to refresh the thinking and teaching practices of the professionals.

RISING EXPECTATIONS

One of the outcomes of working with the emerging digital technology that we all experience is the rising expectation we have of that technology. Initially we are happy to get the gear working and then to make use of all the features. But in time, with competence and confidence, we expect that much more and bemoan the fact that something is a bit slower than normal. When a total teaching staff and student body is using common technology such as an interactive whiteboard or an iPad, their expectations of the technology will grow proportionately.

John Naisbitt (1984), writing in *Megatrends* a quarter of a century ago, identified that the initial move with all new technology is to use it to better perform the ways of old. Over time it is increasingly used for quite different purposes.

When coupling these rising expectations with ever-more sophisticated technology, with thinking networked and with the growing recognition that all teaching and learning does not have to happen in the physical place called school, you will appreciate why you need to be prepared for the ongoing evolution of collaborative teaching.

TIME TO REFLECT

Time is vital to the appropriate evolution—time for teachers to pause and for the school to reflect and ensure it is going in the desired direction. Time is also needed for the community to reflect and consider its role going forward.

The traditional model of school staffing with its strong factory-like origins provides little time for 'the workers' in the classroom to reflect and indeed to contribute to the macro development of the school. The direction setting was vested in the management; the average teacher was disempowered.

One of the great challenges, which you will need to overcome to help the desired evolution, is to find the time and the money needed for the teachers to come together to reflect. That need becomes ever greater when schools go digital and networked, the change becomes constant and increasingly frenetic and you are collaborating with often hundreds of teachers within your community. While it is appreciated that time might be hard to find, it is imperative that you factor it into your planning.

REFINING THE TEACHING

One of the greatest and most challenging tasks, far bigger than any one school can handle, is to identify who best teaches what attributes where. Allied is who best assesses the attainment of those attributes.

Schooling across the developed world works on the seemingly immutable assumption that the only real teaching can be done by professionals working in their classrooms. Most assuredly, those teachers are the only ones trusted to formally assess the students and to do it based on work done in the classroom. Many a teacher union would go spare if you suggested anything else! But as we all know (and as addressed in Chapter 6), that is not so—and increasingly not so in a networked world.

While not for one minute diminishing the important role that is played, and will continue to be played, by the classroom teacher, over time you ought to think about areas where you could markedly enhance the teaching by taking fuller advantage of all the young person's teachers, to personalising aspects and teaching attributes primarily outside the classroom.

Mention has already been made of digital literacy or digital fluency in general. The art of collaboration is another, for globally, while much is made of how vital this skill is, most education authorities do not assess it but continue to focus on solo performance.

You'll soon think of others.

RIDING THE MEGATRENDS

We deliberately left probably the most influential force on the evolving nature of collaborative teaching to the end: the impact that global social and technological megatrends are having and will continue to have.

Once a school appreciates that it can no longer provide the apposite education for a networked world by employing an insular approach to teaching and learning that disregards the global forces, it immediately needs to master the skill of reading the megatrends, of riding those wave-like trends, and knowing when to get off to catch the next. As Mal elaborates in 'Riding the megatrends' (Lee, 2012), this is not a skill the educational leadership literature in general promotes, but it is an imperative today. Annual studies like the Horizon series (Johnson et al., 2010) and the ongoing research by Pew Internet (http://pewinternet.org) offer help.

The aim should be to watch the emerging trends (again using the surfing parlance) like an emerging wave and to decide if or when to get onto that wave. Don't look so much at the now, rather look at the trend lines and, in particular, at trends that are emerging and will impact significantly on the teaching. Some (like the 1:1 computer push promoted by the US computer industry) that are largely artificially generated will be short-lived and soon dissipate. Others, like the shift to highly powerful, multi-purpose personal mobile devices, will be far bigger with a much longer life.

The burgeoning digital and educative capacity of the home, coupled with a diminution of government's ability to fund much of the technology for schools and linked to the integrating force of digital convergence, is a suite of forces that is going to have a profound impact. Just coming on the horizon that will also need watching is the everyday use of artificial intelligence. While the intelligence used with some Android smart phones and Siri being used by Apple is in its infancy, it already has implications for teaching and student assessment. The key is to be proactive and to grasp the opportunities opened.

THE PRAGMATICS OF COLLABORATION

Lastly, in all you do, recognise the pragmatics associated with running a school and accommodating a plethora of linked developments and changes when your school goes digital. The pressures on the teaching staff (of which most parents will be unaware) are likely to be considerable.

One of the more challenging issues you will face will be the teaching and support staff unable to accommodate the new, ever-changing scene. Astute people management and development can sometimes go only so far with staff members who have happily been doing things their way for 20 to 30 years. You may well have to deal with teachers—and often leadership staff—happy to normalise the use of the digital, accepting the general principle of collaboration, but who are unwilling to change their mode of teaching. Changing the teaching style, the pedagogy, of another teacher can be one of the trickiest, most sensitive tasks for in essence one is suggesting to another professional that their teaching is no longer appropriate.

In all the case study situations, the vast majority of the teachers and indeed the professional support embraced the opportunities offered by the collaborative mode, but in many there were also those unwilling to shift to the new. It is a situation you may well encounter.

Bear in mind that in most schools, both government and independent, it is near impossible to dismiss a teacher, in particular one who is simply opting to use a different style of teaching. If there are issues, it is likely to take time to resolve the situation. Some may change their ways, others will seek appointments elsewhere and some might decide that teaching in the networked world, in a world of greater transparency and more collaboration, is not for them. In brief, be prepared to work with a professional teaching and support staff at different degrees of readiness and capacity to accommodate the shift to the more collaborative approach.

CONCLUSION

As you will appreciate, the nature and power of collaboration will evolve at pace—and sometimes at a frightening pace. The not insignificant challenge for you and your school is how you best ready all the teachers for that ever-evolving scene and for them to be comfortable with constant change. The reality, as we flagged earlier, is that there is no ideal model of collaborative teaching; rather, it is about the best possible teaching for the circumstances at a particular point in time. In the next chapter we address the need to astutely measure the effectiveness of the teaching.

CHAPTER **10**

REALISING THE BENEFITS OF COLLABORATION

This chapter draws extensively upon the corporate literature of business realisation and in particular the early shaping ideas of Thorp (1998) contained within *The Information Paradox* and those of Tanner James Consulting Pty Ltd.

SCHOOLS AS COMPLEX ORGANISATIONS

Implementing, monitoring and evaluating change programs in a school are particularly complex at the best of times. In a time when the world around your school is changing rapidly, when new—potentially disruptive—technologies are increasingly accessible, when expectations change constantly, it becomes even more difficult at all stages of the process.

The media, politicians and many of us like to simplify issues, but the reality is that schools working in the networked mode are increasingly complex human organisations whose complexity needs to be understood. That understanding is particularly important when examining the benefits of collaboration inside and outside the school walls. The normalised use of the digital throughout the total school community, and the associated digital convergence, is acting to integrate all facets of the school's operations in a way simply impossible in a paper-based school. But in doing so, it obliges schools in their analysis to appreciate the ever-tighter relationship between the parts and the need to reflect on all the developments from a view up high.

When we say not to over-plan, to allow things to evolve naturally, we do not mean haphazardly with no checks or reviews. Nor do we mean you should not have a very strong sense of where you want your school to get to and why. There should be some sense of a journey's end, even if that is only the start of a new journey! You should also—and, perhaps, most importantly—be very clear about why you are embarking on this journey and what the benefits are for all concerned. Focusing on benefits and their achievement is a positive construct; it keeps the goals of a project firmly to the fore and reminds everyone why they are doing what they are.

For that reason, we have taken the key ideas from the corporate 'benefits realisation' approach and translated them into an educational context. Increasingly, businesses are becoming aware of the need to do more than evaluate the success of a program against desired outcomes. Program management courses such as MSP® (a registered trademark of the Office of Government Commerce in the United Kingdom and other countries) include sections on benefits realisation, ensuring that your overall program achieves the desired result through a range of projects.

Making the desired benefits transparent by clearly defining them, identifying what is needed to achieve them and monitoring their achievement over time is critical to ensuring long-term success for any program. However, schools are arguably more complex than many businesses: there is no one project to implement; there is a complex set of interdependencies to consider; and change is notoriously hard to achieve. For that reason we believe the ideas espoused here are even more important in schools if changes are to be implemented and then sustained—if not built on!

To help you make sense of this chapter, here is a brief explanation of the key terms we will use throughout:

- **Vision**: This is a statement of where you want your school to be and why. It needs to be accessible and relevant to a wide audience; in the case of collaborative teaching, that is, to all teachers of young people, including the young people themselves. It should be the short answer you give whenever anyone asks why you are doing this—or the 'elevator phrases', because it explains things in the time it takes to move between floors!

- **Projects**: These are clearly defined activities with a specific goal. They are focused on one area or outcome; for example, implementing BYOT, implementing a new literacy program or trialling a new timetable. They can be pilots, short-term or long-term. In your school all projects should be clearly linked to the overall vision or strategy you have. They are likely to be one strand in a much larger program.
- **Programs**: These are more complex than projects. They generally involve multiple projects with different outcomes. You probably have an overall program of teaching and learning in your school; you may have a broad program of change that you are implementing. It is within a program of change that the interactions between individual projects and their importance to your overall vision become clear.
- **Outputs**: These are the products of a program; for example, a new literacy unit or a set of laptops.
- **Outcomes**: This is what happens when a program is implemented; for example, teachers use a new set of resources to teach literacy that includes the more frequent use of laptops with their students in class. Through an outcome you are able to realise the desired benefits.
- **Benefits**: These are positive results, or improvements, for one or more groups of people involved in the program; for example, improved scores in literacy results or greater student motivation. Sometimes not everyone sees something as a benefit. In some instances they can even be perceived as dis-benefits by a group of people. Benefits should be measurable.

WHY 'BENEFITS REALISATION'?

Too often when we implement new programs or projects we believe that all we need to do is to ensure we have the necessary capability (technical and human) in place. So we buy new infrastructure, we invest in professional development and then say the project is complete. We do not build iterative development, reflection and refinement into the school's long-term strategic planning. Nor do we look at how different projects link together, how they relate to the overall vision for the school. We do not focus sufficiently beyond the outputs, or even outcomes, to the overall benefits for students.

In the past, the integration of technology has clearly suffered from this issue. Too often governments and schools have followed a 'build it and they will come' implementation model (Ward & Parr, 2011). In this model they have provided (to varying degrees) infrastructure and professional development—both outputs—and then waited for the outcomes and/or benefits to be realised. What they have not done is created the necessary desire for change, or in some instances the necessary capacity. They have not provided good enough reasons for people to do things differently. In these instances, the success of the program is a 'leap of faith' that somehow it will happen.

If there is not a clearly defined benefit that people value, why would they bother to implement—or utilise—something? If you want to work more closely with the other teachers of the young people, everyone needs to see benefit in doing so, and you need to ensure that they can. Just putting the means of communication in place is unlikely to be enough.

Utilising benefits realisation means that all the benefits, to all those involved, are clearly stated from the outset; every step you take is towards realising those—they are the drivers. Making them transparent and reflecting on and reviewing your progress is meaningful and positive. Some projects take you closer to the realisation, but are not on their own sufficient; others are critical steps. Being aware of how everything fits together in a grand plan is vital. You also need to be aware of who may not see benefit in what you are doing, and to manage them (or remove them!).

Evaluating the success (or not) of a program at its conclusion by measuring student outcomes on tests is not enough. Rather, using evidence to inform practice should be continuous across the life cycle of a program and, indeed, in the case of a school, part of business as usual. That evidence should come from a range of sources and include a range of measures of implementation as well as of outcomes. Questions to be considered include:

- Is there sufficient capability on our teaching staff to implement this project?
- Do we have the infrastructure we need?
- Are our teachers, or students, or families making the best use of the infrastructure we have provided?
- Are our parents participating?
- Are we achieving the learning outcomes we want for our students?
- etc.

The tools used to gather evidence can be as simple as asking teachers in a staff meeting, or a simple poll on the school's website, through to a detailed parent survey or analysis of student attendance data over time. Often you can use existing evidence as indicators for other outcomes; for example, attendance = motivation.

Figure 10.1 is an example of a Benefits Realisation cycle leading through to the strategic vision of collaborative teaching. In this instance, the central initiative is the provision of Netbooks in the classroom and related professional training for the teachers.

Outputs *build*
- Netbooks in the classroom
- Teacher professional training

Capability *enables*
- Students have greater access to digital technologies
- Teachers gain greater awareness of how to facilitate their use

Outcomes *realise*
- Classroom practices are adapted to be more open
- Technology is integrated more naturally into the classrooms

Benefits *help achieve*
- Students are better able to create their own knowledge
- Opportunities for learning are extended through access to experts

Strategic vision
- Collaborative teaching

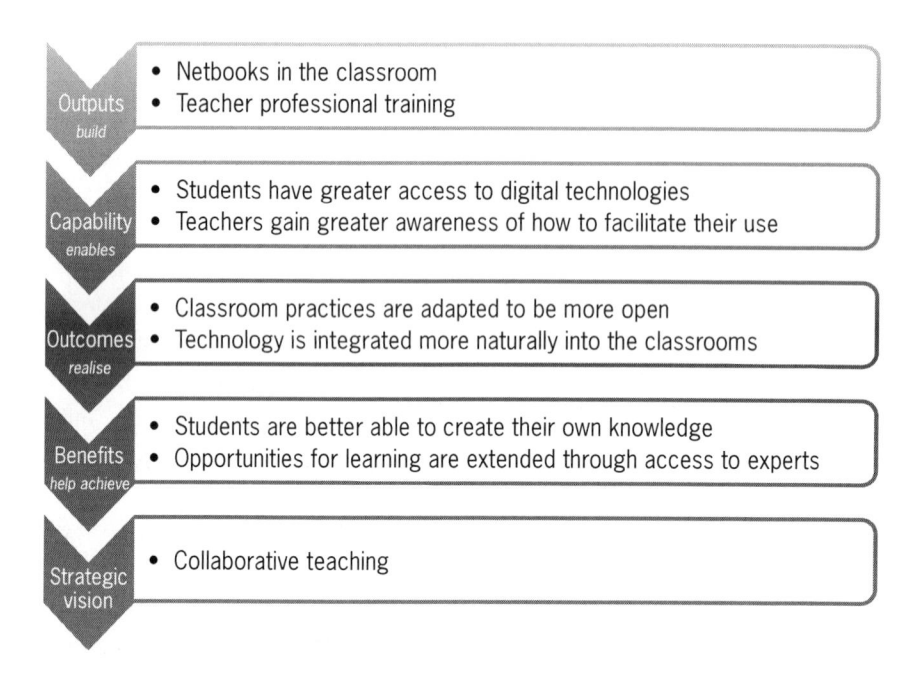

Figure 10.1 *From outputs to benefits*

REALISING BENEFITS THROUGH THE INTEGRATION OF MULTIPLE PROJECTS

How often do you hear teachers say things like 'We did literacy last year, now we are doing digital stuff'? The implication is that literacy was somehow completed and a new project has now started. But how can literacy be 'done'? And surely it is connected to the wider program of teaching and learning in the school? Would not digital technologies be used to enhance literacy outcomes? Does greater use of the digital mean that your literacy program needs to be modified to maximise the potential of the new tools?

In this book, we have often referred to three separate projects that are actually closely linked and are probably symbiotic—they need each other to some extent to succeed. These are BYOT, collaborative teaching and digitalisation of your school. You cannot start and finish these in a neat linear fashion; rather, they need to be juggled, to be managed in a coherent way and revisited and reviewed as circumstances change. Even when you think you have implemented a project, you need to return to it to review whether it is still successful, whether changes are being sustained, whether there is sufficient focus or whether it has been forgotten as the next thing comes along. Figure 10.2 is a diagrammatic depiction of how a range of projects can work together within the one wider program.

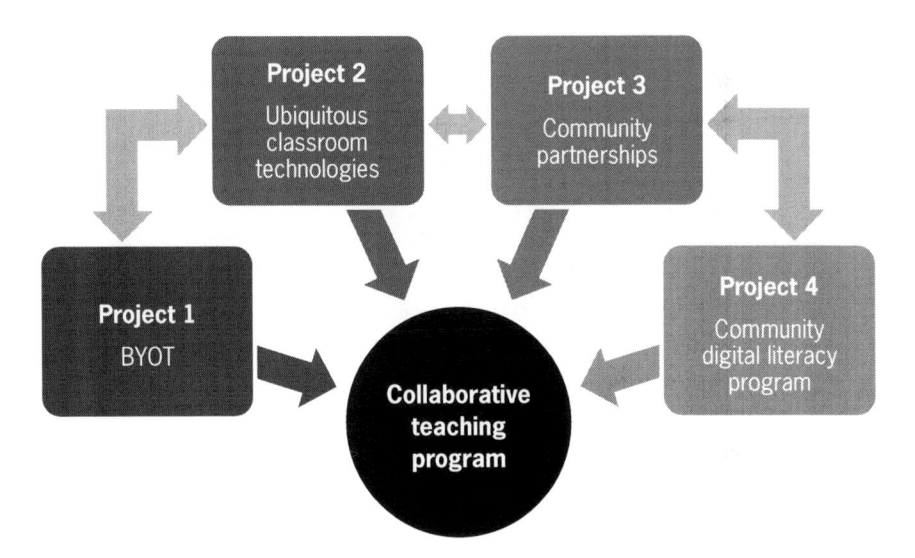

Figure 10.2 Making the connections between projects

The following points are the steps we suggest you should take to ensure that your school focuses on the big-picture outcomes, understands how different projects work together to achieve the desired learning outcomes for your students (and benefits for others in your community) and is able to make decisions based on evidence for the ongoing enrichment of teaching and learning. What we are suggesting here is complex. You may see value in getting some expert help in the early stages to set up an evidence-based program cycle in your school. If you have the capacity on staff or in your community, it would be wise to give that person responsibility for managing the process. They don't need to do it all; they just need to keep a helicopter view and make sure things are happening.

REFLECTING ON YOUR VISION

As stated throughout this book, you need an overall vision for teaching and learning in your school. This vision will drive your overall program of teaching and learning and determine what individual projects you put in place to enable your program.

The vision is likely to be broadly defined and should be aspirational. It will be the touchstone that you return to over time as you review your progress and as you reflect on your journey. As such it cannot be too long; nor should it be a slogan or a motto. It needs to look out to the community and make clear what your school wants to achieve for its learners and what kind of school community you want to be.

Consider your current school vision and ask yourself the following questions:
- Are the benefits of the desired teaching and learning program in your school clearly identifiable from this vision?
- Does the vision speak to the wider school community—all of the teachers and their students?
- Importantly, how long since the vision was revisited? Is it relevant for the networked age? Does it reflect notions of collaborative and connected learners? Is it inclusive of the wider community of teachers?

WHAT WILL HAPPEN WHEN WE IMPLEMENT THE VISION?

While the ultimate benefit of any teaching and learning program is improved outcomes for students, there will be outcomes—positive and negative, intended and unintended—for others in the school community that flow from implementing your vision. Understanding these—mitigating against the negative, preparing for the unintended and promoting the positive—will go a long way towards ensuring the success of your program.

One good way to map this, to make everything transparent, and to reflect on your vision, is to clearly identify all the possible results (outputs, outcomes and benefits) related to implementing your vision. Think about infrastructure, human resources, student learning outcomes, teacher professional development, community learning—and not about just the positive results but also any potential negative side effects (such as increase in teacher workload, greater demands on parents, inequitable access for students who do not have their own devices). Do this as a brainstorming activity and include professional teachers, students and the community. This can be done at an umbrella-program level or for individual projects that you are implementing.

For example, in this book we have suggested that normalising the digital is a necessary step towards realising our vision of collaborative teaching. What are the potential outcomes from doing this?

- increasing integration of digital technologies into classroom practices
- greater demands on the digital devices already in the school
- increased demands on the network due to more devices being used
- a blowout of the school's costs for internet access
- greater student motivation
- greater frustration for teachers and students when things don't work properly
- more awareness in the wider community of what you are doing in the school
- parents feeling pressured to be involved when they don't have time
- teachers feeling threatened as their classrooms are opened to scrutiny
- improved student work because they know there is a public audience
- parental concern about the time their children are spending on the computer
- inequity in outcomes for students
- improved academic outcomes
- inequity in parental involvement as some parents do not have access at home
- savings in stationery costs across the school as less paper and photocopying are required
- fewer textbooks needed for student work
- teachers feeling inadequate to cope with digital literacy requirements
- more effective communication with parents and the wider community
- increased administrative efficiencies
- etc.

Now ask yourselves:
- Which of these are benefits and for whom? Remember benefits are positive changes where the improvements can be measured.
- Are any of them likely to be perceived as dis-benefits and by whom?
- Are some things just outputs and/or outcomes when they should lead to benefits?
- For which of these outcomes do we need to find solutions? These are potential barriers to success; they may be perceptions that need changing or they may require additional infrastructure or some creative use of school resources.
- How do they link together? Do some benefits lead to others? Does more parental involvement lead to better student outcomes?

Some outputs and outcomes obviously lead to benefits in ways that everyone can understand; with others there is more ambiguity. Even today not everyone agrees that digitalisation is an outcome that leads to positive learning benefits!

There may be differing viewpoints even within groups. Some teachers could be excited about the opportunities presented by greater community awareness of what is happening in the school, while others might feel threatened by the opening up of their practices. Some parents want to be involved, while others will see it as an imposition. Being aware of the possible different viewpoints and the need to find solutions for the negative responses, or to neutralise them, is critical to the long-term success of your program.

Use some kind of mind-mapping or graphical representation (lots of butcher paper and coloured pens would be our advice) to map all this out, to make the links and to distinguish the benefits from the problems.

MEASURING THE BENEFITS

Once you are clear on the benefits, how are you going to measure them? You will need a baseline, and then regular evidence gathering and collation. Thinking about the example above, consider the following:
- What evidence do you already collect that can be used as indicators of other things? For example, student attendance records are a measure of motivation as are behaviour records.

- Student achievement data is a given in schools, but can you measure change with what you have?
- What about teacher attitudes? Have you ever surveyed your staff about how they feel about certain things in the school? How do you gauge their motivation, professional knowledge and digital expertise?
- Looking at your school budgets and trends in expenses over time could help you identify where areas of greater cost-efficiency have been achieved. Remember that greater expense in one area could mean less expense overall.

A key point about evidence: it is not just data, not just numbers; it includes observed changes in people's thinking and in their actions; it is about different behaviours and discourses. As long as an improvement can be observed and noted in some way, you have evidence. Make sure you collect some baseline evidence at the start of your journey so that you can see the changes.

MONITOR, REVIEW, EVALUATE AND REFLECT

Collecting evidence is a continuous process—sometimes it is informal and anecdotal, other times it is more organised and intense. There are different levels of evidence gathering and analysis:
- Monitoring, where you track what is happening, looking for trends and changes in patterns; for example, improved student attendance, greater use of the digital tools. This is often done electronically and through graphs.
- Reviewing, where you take stock of what you are doing, thinking about whether it is the right thing or not. This is generally more informal than an evaluation and is a process for checking that you are on the right path. In a review process you would collate the evidence you have gathered and determine whether you are making sufficient progress towards your vision and realising the desired benefits. Some of the questions you would ask are:
    - What capability have we introduced?
    - What changes have we made?
    - Are we closer to realising our desired benefits?
    - Do we have the necessary evidence?
    - What do we need to do differently, if anything?

- Evaluating, which is generally more formal than monitoring or reviewing. It involves measuring the value of a project by determining whether it achieved the desired benefits or not. A good evaluation will also help you understand how those benefits were achieved, or not. It will inform future implementation. This would occur at a major point in your program; for example, when your BYOT project is fully implemented and you want to evaluate its success. Many schools now employ outside experts to undertake evaluations of their projects.

Whichever you choose, remember the 'so what?' Collecting and analysing evidence is only meaningful if it is then acted on; it should not be a compliance activity—something should be learned!

CONCLUSION

There will be times when you just want to sit and reflect, to pause and wonder about what you have done, to remind yourself why you are doing it and where you want to go. Take time to stop, breathe and 'smell the flowers'. When the going gets tough it is critical to reflect on the benefits you are trying to realise. Remind yourself why you are doing this ... reasons sometimes get lost in trivia! And, most importantly, reflect on how far you have come. Look back and celebrate the successes on the way. Sometimes it is only in thinking about where we have come from that we realise how far we have travelled. It can get a little dispiriting if you are looking towards the horizon all the time; seeing how far you have travelled is worth celebrating!

CHAPTER 11

COLLABORATION IN LEARNING: BRINGING IT ALL TOGETHER

The way is now open for any school that wants to move to a mode of teaching apposite for a networked world; that wants to embrace collaboration with those beyond the four walls of a school. For those of you who have already normalised the use of the digital, it is likely that you are already on that journey and many of the points made in this chapter and throughout the book will already be apparent to you. If your school has yet to begin its journey, or is in the very early stages, the path forwards should now be more clearly apparent. In this chapter we reiterate and emphasise the key variables essential for your success in the future.

A VISION FOR COLLABORATION

An effective shaping educational vision for the school and a vision of the kind of collaborative teaching that ultimately you would like the school and its community to provide should be guiding everything you do from here on. The expectation that you provide the best possible teaching for all should underpin that vision. What form the teaching should take and who should teach what, where and at what stage of a young person's development are issues everyone should discuss, explore and refine.

Along the way, and with experience, research and ever-rising teacher, student and parent expectations, the form of that collaboration will likely change, but it is important from the outset to set the expectations high (as we did in Chapter 5). Always put the learner to the fore, but bear in mind much learning is a social experience where interaction with wise teachers will be paramount.

Above all else, don't be afraid to dream your dreams.

NORMALISING THE DIGITAL

Once you have achieved the whole-school, everyday use of the digital in the classroom, your school will move much more naturally to a more collaborative mode of teaching that genuinely involves all the teachers of the young people. The experience of the case studies suggests that the normalisation of the digital often simultaneously prompts schools to also use the students' own mobile technology in the class (BYOT) and to adopt a model of school technology support that focuses on facilitating the pertinent use of the students' technology rather than, as is still the case today, tightly controlling the use of school-acquired technology.

Significantly, all three developments—the normalisation of the digital, BYOT and collaborative teaching—work to position the learner, and not the teacher, to the fore. They support the personalisation of both the learning and the learning environment.

While it is vital that all three developments are allowed to grow and evolve naturally, if your school and its community are to maximise the educational potential of collaboration there is a need for school leaders to consciously nurture, shape, support and constantly refine the developments within their own context. The challenge is to take a raw, largely unformed natural development and to transform it into a mode of teaching and learning befitting an increasingly sophisticated networked world.

In Chapter 8 we highlighted a method for walking this line between a structured change plan and a more flexible and responsive evolution of teaching and learning. Maintaining this balance is critical. Evolution doesn't mean change in any direction; it simply means being willing and able to alter that direction as necessary.

A VISIONARY LEADER IS VITAL

A principal who is willing and able to lead, who constantly expects the most from all the teachers of the young people is critical for all schools. We cannot emphasise enough the need for a visionary leader, one who can observe the new trends, make valid judgements about trends that are suitable for their school and who can motivate and encourage others. The need to gain the support of the wider community is vital for the success of any collaborative initiative. The role of the leadership and its central importance should be clear.

THE IMPORTANCE OF SUPPORTING THE PROFESSIONAL TEACHERS

The key role to be played by all the school's professional educators, albeit different and in many respects more difficult, should also be clear. The shift to a more collaborative model will take them into a style of teaching and learning where few have travelled, where none have traversed the full distance and where much has yet to be learned.

While placing the needs of the individual student to the fore and personalising the teaching will come easily for the parents and their children, it will invariably require a significant shift in the thinking and teaching of most teachers. It won't happen overnight and will entail significant support. So, too, will the idea that the teaching and learning can and should happen anywhere, any time, 24/7/365.

It will take time to shake off the very strong inclination of many professional teachers to return to a mass 'one size fits all' solution and to accept a diversity of approaches as one personalises the student teaching and learning. In the case study schools that have opted for a model of BYOT, it is fascinating to note teachers coming to grips with the use of different types of technology and operating systems in their teaching.

As mentioned upfront, a related reality is that while collaborative teaching seems such a logical and natural approach, a mode of teaching that involves a team of people working in harmony inside and outside the school walls in an ever-evolving environment will be significantly more complex and challenging than that we have all known. Embracing collaboration requires an ever-more sophisticated and holistic understanding of the teaching and learning process. It obliges teachers to employ a skill set and exercise a facility to accommodate ongoing, often rapid and uncertain, change which some of the present teachers might not have. The case study experience suggests there may well be teachers in your school, even with the best support and training, who believe themselves unable to survive in the new situation. It is a very big ask of the professional teachers, and while most will find the experience to be immensely rewarding and exciting (as have the case study schools), the reality is that you may have teachers so terrified of venturing into the unknown and leaving their comfort zone that they will choose to retire or leave the profession. Even worse, despite the best efforts of the school leadership, some may choose to put their heads in the sand, close the classroom door and try to pretend nothing is happening. (These are the ones who may need to be gently pushed towards the door!)

It is important that all within the school's community understand the load the move towards a more collaborative model places on the professionals, and why it so important that they are offered support. Unnecessary burdens, such as the often inordinate amount of 'administrivia' and accountability testing found in many jurisdictions, must be minimised.

SUPPORT OF AND FOR THE OTHER TEACHERS

Gaining the support of the non-professional teachers (particularly the parents) and supporting them as they increasingly become active participants in the learning of the young people is also critical. While, as mentioned, all the case study situations are seeking to provide the home with appropriate support, the reality is that it will take time, discussion, reflection, school-ground chats (and possibly some heated words!) before the bulk of parents attune themselves to the more collaborative teaching model. A skill like metacognition cannot be learnt overnight. If in time parents are rightly involved in the assessment of certain student skills, the art of doing so will need to be refined.

The same holds with the students and their desire to make wise use of self- and peer teaching. There is the very real likelihood (being conscious of the fact that few educators contemplate students also being teachers) that initially it could be the young person explaining to the professional teacher the nature of self- and peer teaching, but in time all professional educators should have a sophisticated understanding of both forms of teaching and be able to assist their students in using them astutely.

Regardless of all we have said, the physical classroom will continue for many years yet to be the key place of teaching, particularly of the academic curriculum, and the professional educator will and should continue to be the young people's lead teacher of the academic, and play a leading role in assisting and supporting the other teachers in the development of the other key educational building blocks.

That support and development has to be a normal part of the school's everyday operations evolving as the school and its communities become more sophisticated. The professional teachers have the expertise and time to play a lead role, and indeed will be expected by society to take prime operational responsibility. They ought to be the ones who anticipate the educational expectations of the parents and the support that is needed.

In brief, all the teachers of our young people, not simply the classroom teacher, will need to be provided with appropriate ongoing support, time and training, and the chance to reflect and refine their teaching. And all should be expected to teach their area(s) of responsibility as best they can.

PUTTING THE BENEFITS AT THE CENTRE

As we discussed in Chapter 10, one way of ensuring you both guide the evolution of your school and win the support of your school community is to use the ideas of benefits realisation. By ensuring everyone is aware of why you are doing what you are doing and of the benefits to be gained, you can develop a system of monitoring and review that ensures the end goal is always in sight.

Checking on progress against the attainment of benefits is one way of ensuring your program has not gone astray, that you are still heading in the right general direction. You also need to check that you have the appropriate support structures in place. It is also a good way of reminding everyone why they are doing what they are doing and, importantly, how much they have achieved. At times it may be opportune to rest and for the school to catch its breath before continuing with the journey.

The facility to clarify and refine your vision should become that much easier when all the teachers of the young people—professionals and non-professionals—are that much more comfortable thinking within a networked mindset and considering solutions appropriate for the school at a particular phase in its evolution as well as for each student therein.

IT WON'T BE EASY AND IT WILL TAKE TIME

The ongoing refinement and embedding of the collaborative teaching concept will take time. While it is important to dream the dreams and to have high expectations, it is also important to appreciate that you will be developing the model in a working school with all its inevitable everyday dramas. Even with the best preparations and general widespread acceptance and excitement, there are going to be instances where the development will be tested, where a teacher new to the school refuses to change, where an over-enthusiastic parent alienates the teachers and where a bureaucrat imposes a solution alien to what your school is about.

That is the normality of schooling. It is one of the many reasons why you need that capable principal—and why they should be so well paid!

Schooling is already a highly complex human endeavour. Add to the mix all the teachers of young people and a 24/7/365 approach that more consciously seeks to shape the learning in the current untouched 80 per cent time, and you have an ever-more complex organisation. In making the move to the more collaborative teaching it is thus imperative that the school has in place highly efficient systems that make good use of the technology to ensure all operations, both inside and outside the school walls, are tightly integrated and linked seamlessly. You are going to need good people if you are to realise the immense potential of this move and to finally provide each of your learners with the appropriate education.

CONCLUSION

As indicated at the outset, our desire with this book was to alert all associated with the schooling of the nation's young people, teachers and parents alike, of a major natural transformation in the nature of teaching that is underway across the developed world. We wanted to flesh out its likely potential and the openings it provides to markedly enhance the teaching and learning of all young people in an increasingly sophisticated world, where the use of the digital has become normalised and, in Shirky's words, is fast becoming invisible, and where the divisions of old are fast disappearing.

At this still early phase of the journey we don't pretend to have all the answers to the best way forward, but already we feel sufficiently comfortable to posit that collaborative teaching will be the teaching mode of a networked world.

Enjoy your journey.

We would be delighted to learn how you go. If at any stage you want to share your experiences, do write to Lorrae at lorrae@cyperus.co.nz or Mal at mallee@mac.com.

BIBLIOGRAPHY

Australian Communications and Media Authority (ACMA) 2007, *Media and communications in Australian families*, ACMA, Canberra. Available from http://www.acma.gov.au/webwr/_assets/main/lib101058/media_and_society_report_2007.pdf.
Australian Institute of Family Studies (AIFS) 2007, 'A snapshot of how Australian families spend their time', AIFS, Canberra. Available from http://www.aifs.gov.au/institute/pubs/snapshots/familytime.html.
Berthelsen, D 2010, 'Support at home increases chance of school success', *Science Network*, Insciences Organisation. Available from http://insciences.org/article.php?article_id=2319.
Berthelsen, D & Walker, S 2008, 'Parents' involvement in their children's education', *Family Matters*, vol. 79.
Betcher, C & Lee, M 2009, *The interactive whiteboard revolution: Teaching with IWBs*, ACER Press, Camberwell.
Bolstadt, R & Lin, M 2009, *Students' experiences of learning in virtual classrooms*, New Zealand Council for Educational Research (NZCER). Report prepared for the Ministry of Education, Wellington.
Chansanchai, A 2011, 'Kindle books now outsell paperbacks', *Technolog*, NCBNews.com. Available from http://technolog.msnbc.msn.com/_news/2011/01/28/5940731-kindle-books-now-outsell-paperbacks.
Cohn, D 2007, 'Do parents spend enough time with their children?', Population Reference Bureau. Available from http://www.prb.org/Articles/2007/DoParentsSpendEnoughTimeWithTheirChildren.aspx.
Cowan, RJ, Swearer Napolitano, SM & Sheriden, SM 2004, *Home–school collaboration*, University of Nebraska Educational Psychology Papers and Publications Paper 18, Department of Educational Psychology, University of Nebraska, Lincoln.
De Carvalho, ME 2001, *Rethinking family–school relations: A critique of parental involvement in schooling*, Lawrence Erlbaum Associates, Philadelphia.
Deacon, S 2011, *Joining the dots: A better start for Scotland's children*, University of Edinburgh. Available from http://www.scotland.gov.uk/Resource/Doc/343337/0114216.pdf.
Demski, J 2012, '7 Habits of Highly Effective Tech-leading Principals', *The Journal*, 6 July 2012. Available from http://thejournal.com/Articles/2012/06/07/7-habits-of-highly-effective-tech-leading-principals.aspx?Page=1.
Desforges, C & Abouchaar, A 2003, *The impact of parental involvement, parent support and family education on pupil achievement and adjustment: A literature review*, Nottingham Department for Education and Skills, Research Report RR433.
Drucker, P 2001, *Management challenges for the 21st century*, HarperCollins, New York.
Eckert, P 1989, *Jocks and burnouts: Social categories and identity in the high school*, Teachers College Press, New York.
Estyn 2009, *Good practice in parental involvement in primary schools—April 2009*, Her Majesty's Inspectorate for Education and Training, Cardiff, Wales.
Friedman, T 2006, *The world is flat*, 2nd edn, Farrar, Straus Giroux, New York.
Gee, JP 2007, *What video games have to teach us about learning and literacy*, 2nd edn,

Palgrave Macmillan, New York.

Gonzalez-deHass, AR & Willems, RP 2003, 'Examining the underutilization of parent involvement in the schools', *The School Community Journal*, vol. 13, no. 1, pp. 85–100. Available from http://www.adi.org/journal/ss03/gonzalez-dehass%20 &%20willems.pdf.

Grant, D 1989, *Learning relations*, Routledge, London.

Grant, L 2010a (August), *Developing the home–school relationship using digital technologies*, Futurelab. Available from http://www.futurelab.org.uk/resources/ developing-home-school-relationship-using-digital-technologies-handbook.

Grant, L 2010b (December), *Connecting digital literacy between home and school*, Futurelab. Available from http://www.futurelab.org.uk/resources/connecting-digital-literacy-between-home-and-school.

Green, H & Hannon, C 2007, *Their space: Education for a digital generation*, Demos, London.

Hansen, MT 2009, *Collaboration: How leaders avoid the traps, create unity and reap big results*, Harvard University Press, Boston.

Hart, B & Risley, T 1999, *The social world of children: Learning to talk*, Paul H. Brookes Publishing, Baltimore.

Hattie, J 2009, *Visible learning*, Routledge, London.

Hirst, PH 1971, 'What is teaching?', *Journal of Curriculum Studies*, vol. 3, pp. 5–18.

Isaacson, W 2011, *Steve Jobs*, Simon & Schuster, New York.

Ito, M, Horst, H, Bittanti, M, Boyd, d, Herr-Stephenson, B, Lange, P, Pascoe, C & Robinson, L 2008, *Living and learning with new media: Summary of findings from the Digital Youth Project*, The John D and Catherine T Macarthur Foundation Reports on Digital Media and Learning. Available from http://digitalyouth. ischool.berkeley.edu/files/report/digitalyouth-WhitePaper.pdf.

Johnson, L, Levine, A, Smith, R & Stone S 2010, *The 2010 Horizon Report*, The New Media Consortium, Austin, Texas.

Lee, M 2010 (July), 'Interactive whiteboards and schooling: The context', *Technology, Pedagogy and Education*, vol. 19. no. 2, pp. 133–41.

Lee, M & Finger, G (eds) 2010, *Developing a networked school community: A guide to realising the vision*, ACER Press, Camberwell.

Lee, M & Gaffney, M 2008, *Leading a digital school*, ACER Press, Camberwell.

Lee, M & Hough, M 2011, 'Involving the nation's grandparents in the schooling of its young'. Available from malleehome.com/?p=143.

Lee, M & Levins, M 2012, *Bring Your Own Technology: The BYOT guide for schools and families*, ACER Press, Camberwell.

Lee, M & Ward, L 2012a, 'Collaborative teaching'. Available from http://malleehome. com/?p=180.

Lee, M & Ward, L 2012b, 'Managing school development and performance in the networked mode'. Available from http://malleehome.com/wp-content/ uploads/2010/09/Managing-School-Development.doc.

Lee, M & Winzenried, A 2009, *The use of instructional technology in schools: Lessons to be learned*, ACER Press, Camberwell.

Levy, R 2009, 'You have to understand words … but not read them: Young children becoming readers in a digital age', *Journal of Research in Reading*, vol. 32, no. 1, pp. 75–91. Available from http://onlinelibrary.wiley.com/doi/10.1111/j.1467-9817.2008.01382.x/pdf.

Lipnack, J & Stamps, J 1994, *The age of the network: Organizing principles for the 21st century*, John Wiley & Sons, New York.

BIBLIOGRAPHY

Mackenzie, J 2009, *Family learning: Engaging with parents*, Dunedin Academic Press, Edinburgh.

Meredyth, D, Russell, N, Blackwood, L, Thomas, J & Wise, P 1998, *Real time: Computers, change and schooling*, Department of Education, Training and Youth Affairs, Canberra.

Naisbitt, J 1984, *Megatrends*, Futura, London.

NCREL 2011, 'High Expectations', North Central Regional Educational Laboratory. Available from http://www.ncrel.org/sdrs/areas/issues/students/atrisk/at6lk11.htm.

OECD 1997, *Parents as partners in schooling*, Organisation for Economic Co-operation and Development, Paris.

OECD 2012, 'Are boys and girls ready for the digital age?', *PISA in focus*, 12, Organisation for Economic Co-operation and Development, Paris. Available from http://www.oecd.org/pisa/49442737.pdf.

Parr, JM & Ward, L 2010, *Laptops for teachers evaluation*, Report to the Ministry of Education, Wellington, New Zealand, UniServices, University of Auckland.

Patrikakou, E 2004, 'Adolescence: Are parents relevant to student's high school achievement and post-secondary attainment?', (Family Involvement Research Digest), Harvard Family Research Project, Cambridge, MA. Available from http://www.hfrp.org/publications-resources/browse-our-publications/adolescence-are-parents-relevant-to-students-high-school-achievement-and-post-secondary-attainment.

Prensky, M 2006, *Don't bother me Mom—I'm learning!*, Paragon House, St Paul, Minnesota.

Project Tomorrow 2010, *Unleashing the future: Educators 'speak up' about the use of emerging technologies for learning*, Speak Up May 2010, Project Tomorrow. www.tomorrow.org.

Project Tomorrow 2011, *The new three E's of education: Enabled, engaged and empowered*, Speak Up 2010, National Findings Project Tomorrow. www.tomorrow.org.

Project Tomorrow 2012, *Personalizing the classroom experience: Teachers, librarians and administrators connect the dots with digital learning*, Speak Up May 2012, National Findings Project Tomorrow. Available from http://www.tomorrow.org/speakup/SU11_PersonalizedClassroom_EducatorsReport.html.

Shirky, C 2008, *Here comes everybody: Organizing without organizations*, Penguin, New York.

Singer, D & Singer, J 2005, *Imagination and play in the electronic era*, Harvard University Press, Cambridge, Massachusetts.

Sparks, SD 2011 (August), 'Statistics show more grandparents caring for grandchildren', *Education Week*.

Strom, RD & Strom, PS 2010, *Parenting young children: Exploring the Internet, play and reading*, Information Age Publishing, Charlotte.

Tapscott, D 1998, *Growing up digital: The rise of the Net Generation*, McGraw Hill, New York.

Tapscott, D 2009, *Grown up digital: How the Net Generation is changing our world*, McGraw Hill, New York.

Tharp, R & Gallimore, R 1991, *The instructional conversation: Teaching and learning in social activity Research Report 2*, The National Center for Research on Cultural Diversity and Second Language Learning, University of California, Santa Cruz, California. Available from http://escholarship.org/uc/item/5th0939d.

Thorp, J 1998, *The information paradox*, McGraw Hill, Toronto.

Tyack, D & Tobin, W 1994, 'The grammar of schooling: Why has it been so hard to change?', *American Research Journal*, vol. 31, no. 3, pp. 453–79.

Valsiner, J 1997, *Culture and the development of children's actions: A theory of human development*, 2nd edn, John Wiley & Sons, Chichester.

Vause, L & Cameron, L 2012, 'CLC (Collaborative Learning Community)—Initiated action research as a means to teacher development'. Paper presented at the Annual Meeting of the American Educational Research Association, Vancouver.

Wagaman, J 2011, 'Teaching children self-control has long-term benefits', Parenting Resources, Suite 101. Available from http://www.suite101.com/content/teaching-children-self-control-has-long-term-benefits-a338053.

Ward, L 2012, 'Creating a richer educational environment: Digital bridges and virtual islands'. Available from http://www.malleehome.com/?page_id=51.

Ward, L & Henderson, A 2011, *Network learning communities evaluation*. Main report to the Ministry of Education, Wellington, New Zealand, Cyperus Ltd.

Ward, L & Marentette, P 2012, 'The NEN Trial Evaluation Report series', Ministry of Education, New Zealand.

Ward, L & Parr, J 2011, 'Digitalising our schools: Clarity and coherence in policy', *Australian Journal of Educational Technology*, vol. 27, no. 2, pp. 326–42. Available from http:// www.ascilite.org.au/ajet/ajet27/ward.html.

Ward, L, Robinson, VMJ & Parr, JM 2005, 'Getting ICT into classrooms: The case for broader swamps in the future', *Computers in New Zealand Schools*, vol. 17, no. 2, pp. 23–9.

Weare, K & Gray, G 2003, 'What works in developing children's emotional and social competence and wellbeing', Department for Education Research Report RR456, Department for Education. Available from http://www.education.gov.uk/rsgateway/DB/RRP/u014091/index.shtml.

Wenger, E 1998, *Communities of practice: Learning, meaning and identity*, Cambridge University Press, Cambridge.

INDEX

Apiti   17, 25, 35, 36, 40, 60, 68, 77, 85, 93
authentic experiences   35, 124

Balmacewen   17, 23, 26, 34, 35, 36, 37, 41, 124
benefits   vii, 3, 4, 13, 22, 34, 40, 41, 48, 52, 59, 60, 74, 75, 80, 81, 86, 91, 102–112, 117
   dis-benefits   104, 110, 124
   synergy   89, 124
   unintended benefits   60, 108, 124
benefits realisation approach   102–112
Broulee Public School   17, 25, 29, 33, 34, 38, 40, 41, 60, 64, 85
BYOT   ii, 24, 26, 34, 40, 52, 61, 62, 83, 87, 104, 107, 112, 114, 115
   normalisation   52, 59, 61

case study schools   xiv, 4, 7, 8, 15–19, 21–30, 32, 41, 48, 49, 50, 51, 57, 61, 64, 68, 69, 77, 78, 80, 81, 83, 84, 85, 86, 87, 88, 91, 94, 97, 100, 115, 116, 124
   findings   18–19, 21–30, 61
change   4, 6, 7, 13, 20, 22, 25, 28, 29, 30, 41, 44, 45, 49, 54, 55, 58, 61, 66, 67, 68, 69, 71, 73, 75, 76, 79, 80, 90, 92, 94, 96, 100, 101, 102, 103, 104, 107, 110, 111, 114, 118
Coal Mountain Elementary   17, 60, 83, 124
collaboration   vii, 1, 2, 3–28, 32–38, 40, 41, 43, 44, 46, 48–49, 52, 54, 57, 58, 59, 61, 64, 66, 67, 69, 73, 72, 79, 80, 81, 84, 85, 86, 88, 89, 90, 94, 96, 98, 102, 107, 110, 113, 114, 115–117, 118, 119
   authentic   6, 9, 35, 36, 124
   with community   vii, 1, 2, 3–28, 32–38, 40, 41, 43, 44, 46, 48–49, 52, 54, 57, 58, 59, 61, 64, 66, 67, 69, 73, 72, 79, 80, 81, 84, 85, 86, 88, 89, 90, 94, 96, 98, 102, 107, 110, 113, 114, 115–117
   with families   11, 38–40, 57, 62
   with other professionals   2, 5, 15, 28, 37, 38, 67, 68, 79, 81, 84, 89, 98, 116
   with other schools   39
collaboration in learning wheel   46
collaborative teaching   vii, ix, 1, 3, 4, 6, 7, 8, 9, 10–13, 20, 21, 23, 25, 27, 29, 32, 33, 35, 40, 43–51, 52–65, 66–78, 79–91, 100
   benefits   4, 13, 22, 34, 40, 41, 52, 48, 59–64, 74, 75, 86, 102–112
   definition   10–11, 44–45
   nature   1, 3, 4, 6, 7, 8, 9, 10–13, 20, 21, 23, 25, 27, 29, 32, 33, 35, 40, 43–51, 52–65
   potential teachers   53–59
   vision   3, 4, 43–51
community—*see* teachers
Concordia College   38, 39, 64, 93
context
   school specific solutions   12, 15, 23, 28, 32, 44, 46, 86, 94, 114
Corpus Christi   17
culture   19, 23, 32, 37, 41, 57, 73
current situation   5–31

digital communication suite   24, 25, 28, 34, 85, 88, 95
digital empowerment—*see* empowerment
digital normalisation—*see* normalisation of the digital
digital schooling   vi, 3, 4, 5–9, 18, 25, 59, 62, 92, 98
digital technologies   2, 8, 24–25, 38, 46, 69, 70, 71, 74, 106, 107, 109
dismantling school walls   9, 10, 11, 13, 26–27

early adopters/pathfinders   vi, 2, 12, 13, 15, 16, 21–31, 32, 50, 69, 71, 78, 91
early digital phase   6, 8, 9, 17, 18
early networked phase   6, 8, 9, 17, 18
educational context—*see* context
empowerment   55, 95–96
   digital   55
   parents   55, 96
   teachers   55, 96
equity   72, 73, 109

INDEX

evolution   vii, ix, 4, 5–9, 16, 19–20, 49, 50, 64, 89, 90, 92–93, 94, 95, 96, 97, 98, 114, 117
 BYOT   24, 34, 40, 52, 59, 61, 83, 87, 107
 natural   41, 64, 82–83
 of schooling   vii, ix, 4, 5, 7–9, 64, 92–93, 96
 school technology support model   58, 70, 84

Forsyth Central High School   17
Forsyth County School District   28, 30, 83, 85, 87, 90, 91
Friends School, The   11, 17, 38, 41, 60, 93

home–school collaboration   vi, 2, 3, 4–5, 7, 8, 9, 23, 24, 25, 27, 33, 34, 35, 52–65, 68, 83–84, 87
 impact   33, 34, 35, 52–65
 nexus—*see* home–school collaboration
 rarity   2–3, 4–5
 recognition   52, 53, 54, 55–56, 59–60
 resources   33–34
home–school divide   vi, 5, 12, 13
 bridging the divide   62–63

impact
 potential   v, 7, 28, 49, 51, 60, 62, 85, 90, 99, 100
implementation   21, 32, 48, 66–78, 79–91, 104, 105, 112
 first steps   12–13, 79–82
 graduated   85–86
 launch   86–87
 principles   66–78
integration   3, 33, 34, 52, 71, 89, 94, 104, 106

Kim Ora   17, 37, 38

megatrends   93, 97, 99
methodology   14–19
Mount Hobson   17, 26, 34, 35, 36, 38, 40, 84
multi-purpose operations   27, 99

networked mindset   13, 34, 68, 69, 89, 94, 95, 117
networked school communities   1, 2, 6, 12, 13, 18, 19, 30, 37, 47, 67, 83, 85, 117
networks   8, 11, 95
Noadswood School   17, 28, 60, 64, 77, 85, 93
normalisation of the digital   43, 68–71, 74–75, 114
 importance   43, 68–71

outcomes   vii, 1, 11, 12, 28, 29, 43, 48, 67, 76, 83, 94, 97, 103–110
outputs   vii, 104–106, 109–110

paper-based schooling   3, 8, 9, 57, 59, 62, 92
planning   61, 78, 79, 80, 83, 87, 94, 98, 104
 natural evolution and growth—*see* evolution
 over-planning   83
 strategic   80–81
principal   6, 7, 21, 22, 27, 33, 34, 36, 40, 67, 68, 71, 73, 74, 75, 77, 93, 94, 115, 118
programs   34, 40, 60, 64, 97, 102, 104
professional development—*see* support and training
Project Tomorrow   10, 54, 55, 58, 76
projects   34, 36, 40, 103–112
promotion   86–87
Pukeokahu   17, 25, 27, 34, 36, 85, 93

rationale   40, 52–65, 79, 95
readiness   20, 66–78, 80, 100
 infrastructure   87–88
 parents   76–78
 school   67–72
 students   76
 teachers   70–71, 74–75
 technological   68–69, 87–88
refinement   63, 81, 89–90, 91, 92–101, 104, 118
reflection   19, 32, 41, 53, 92, 98, 104, 116

school educational vision   vi, 19, 21–22, 25, 40, 79, 80, 81–82, 92, 103, 104,

125

INDEX

106, 108, 109, 111, 113, 115, 117
school leadership   16, 19, 21–22, 27, 28, 29, 41, 64, 68, 70, 73, 74, 80, 86, 90, 91, 99, 100, 115, 116
school resourcing   34, 52, 59
South Forsyth High School   17, 60, 83
student attainment   4, 10, 40, 59–60, 93, 98, 117
support and training   28, 41, 57, 64, 70, 78, 84–85, 89, 97, 116–117
sustained evolution and development

teachers   vi, vii, 1–5, 6, 7, 8, 10–14, 18, 20, 22, 23, 24, 27, 28, 33, 34, 35, 37–39, 43–51, 52–60, 62, 63, 64, 66, 67, 68, 69, 70, 71, 74, 75, 77, 78, 81, 82, 83, 84, 89, 90, 92, 95–97, 98, 100, 115–117, 118
   community   vii, 1–7, 11, 12, 13, 16, 18, 19, 20, 21, 23, 24, 25, 28, 32, 33–35, 36–41, 43–44, 46, 48, 49, 52–65, 66, 67, 72, 73, 74–78, 79, 80, 82, 84, 85, 86, 88, 89, 91, 94, 95, 96, 98, 102, 107, 109, 110, 113–117
   elders   24, 33, 57, 59, 78, 84
   empowerment—*see* empowerment
   grandparents   2, 5, 9, 33, 40, 46, 53, 56, 57, 59, 64, 76, 77, 78, 84, 85, 89, 96, 97
   non-professional   11, 116–117
   parents   53–56
   professional   37–39, 96–97, 115–116
   readiness   23, 73–78
   students   39, 57–59
   willingness to collaborate   74–78
teaching   viii, 2, 3, 4, 5, 6, 7, 8, 9, 10, 11, 12, 13, 16, 20, 22, 23, 25, 27, 28, 29, 32, 35, 37, 38, 39, 42, 47, 49, 51, 53, 55, 57–59, 60, 61–63, 64, 66, 67, 68, 69–71, 75, 77, 80, 83, 84, 89, 91, 93, 96–97, 98–99, 100, 101, 106, 107, 108–110, 114, 116–118
   collaborative—*see* collaborative teaching
   digitally based   6, 7, 8, 9, 69–71, 77, 114
   enhancement   33–34, 63–64, 108–110

insular paper based   3, 6, 8, 9, 10, 28, 43, 49, 66, 68, 92
outside classroom   9, 10, 11, 13, 26–27, 32, 35, 37, 38, 39, 47, 50, 51, 53, 55, 56, 60, 61, 62–64, 83–84, 96–97, 116–117
personalised   59, 61–62
self   4, 57–59
24/7/365   5, 10, 11, 26–27, 34, 35, 51, 80, 84, 93, 115
technology   v, 5, 7, 9, 10, 12, 24, 27, 33, 34, 35, 49, 50, 52, 53, 55, 57, 58, 59, 61, 62, 64, 70, 71, 73, 76, 77, 83, 84, 85, 87, 94, 95, 97, 98, 99, 104, 72, 106, 114, 118
transcending classroom walls—*see* dismantling school walls
trust   23, 77, 98

Zone theory of development   46, 116

Bring Your Own Technology

The BYOT guide for schools and families

Mal Lee and Martin Levins

In time, all schools in the developed world will move to students using their personal mobile technology in class, rather than it being provided by the school. It is not a case of if, but when.

The forces impelling the change and the potential educational, social, economic, technological and political opportunities opened by the development will soon fundamentally change the nature of schooling, teaching, the technology used, home–school relations and the resourcing of schools.

BYOT is far more than a technological change. However, its full potential will only be realised by schools, their leadership and their communities collaborating astutely to achieve the normalised 100% student use of the technology.

This book, drawing on the work of the pathfinding schools and education authorities in the UK, the USA and Australia, is designed to provide teachers and parents alike an insight into:

- why the development needs to be embraced
- the imperative of authentic collaboration between home and school
- what each school needs to do to ready itself
- how to deal with the raft of options
- the kinds of whole school community implementation strategy required
- the practicalities of achieving sustained total student usage and the many dividends that will then flow.

sales@acer.edu.au | 03 9277 5447 | Order online: http://shop.acer.edu.au
www.acer.edu.au/publications/education

Leading a Digital School

Principles and practice

Edited by Mal Lee and Michael Gaffney

This important book informs educational leaders about current developments in the use of digital technologies and presents a number of case studies demonstrating their value and complexity. It encourages leaders to engage in the process of successful change for their own school community by providing guidelines and advice drawn from emerging research.

Leading a Digital School is a rich source of information and advice about joining the 'education revolution'. It shows clearly and concisely how schools can integrate digital technologies creatively and wisely in order to enliven teaching and support student learning.

Developing a Networked School Community

A guide to realising the vision

Edited by Mal Lee and Glenn Finger

In the 20th century, school was the place you went to learn; in the 21st century, because of digital technologies, children learn things at home which they don't or aren't allowed to at school. This makes the relationship between school, home and the community even more important than previously. Schools need to recognise this and use it to advantage. Schools, educational leaders and bureaucrats need to overcome their fear of digital technologies and embrace the challenge and opportunities.

This book is the first major work which defines and explores the concept of the Networked School Community and details the challenges and opportunities of its implementation from the perspective of the system, the school, the teacher, the student, the home, and the parent.

sales@acer.edu.au | 03 9277 5447 | Order online: http://shop.acer.edu.au
www.acer.edu.au/publications/education

The Interactive Whiteboard Revolution

Teaching with IWBs

Chris Betcher and Mal Lee

Interactive whiteboards are not just another classroom technology. As the first digital technology designed specifically for teaching and learning, they have the potential to radically alter the way we learn. IWBs also facilitate the integration and ready use of all other digital technologies — hardware and software. Just as the blackboard was the symbol and transformative technology of the 19th century classroom, the interactive whiteboard is the centrepiece of the 21st century digital classroom.

The Use of Instructional Technology in Schools

Lessons to be learned

Mal Lee and Arthur Winzenried

The Use of Instructional Technology in Schools examines teachers' use of the major instructional technologies over the last century — from the days of silent film, radio and slide shows through to the modern interactive whiteboard and the internet. It explores the reasons why so few teachers have used these technologies and why, even in today's digital world, the most commonly used classroom tools are the pen, paper and teaching board.

The book provides decision makers with an invaluable insight into the million dollar question: What is required to get all teachers across the nation using the appropriate instructional technology as a normal part of everyday teaching? Without question, student learning is enhanced by adopting these new technologies.

sales@acer.edu.au | 03 9277 5447 | Order online: http://shop.acer.edu.au
www.acer.edu.au/publications/education